Learn French?
Of Course You Can!

OTHER PUBLICATIONS OF *LANGUAGES AT HOME*

Books

Travelling in France: Essential Communication for the Smart Tourist (available in print format, and as an e-book with audio links): An easy guide of everyday French expressions and vocabulary indispensable for foreigners travelling in France (2016).

Say It With a French Accent (e-book): Grammar explanations and audio scenarios.

Live Like a French Person (e-book): Audio scenarios on daily life in France.

Grammar French Basics (e-book): The basics of French grammar, explained in English, for beginners.

Raise Your Children With a French Accent (e-book): Audio scenarios on children's daily life; songs and stories.

Write Like a French Person (e-book): A compilation of dictations, for beginners and intermediary French students, with audio links.

Cook Like a French Person (e-book): A bilingual selection of French recipes.

Magazines

French Accent Magazine: Published every two months, the essential e-magazine for French learners, with a central theme, articles on various topics such as politics, culture and literature, grammar, scenarios and vocabulary with audio links.

More details on all publications: www.frenchaccentmagazine.com

Learn French?
Of Course You Can!

The First Self-Help Guide For French Learners

By the founders of *Languages at Home*
and editors of *French Accent Magazine*

© 2016 by *Learn Languages at Home*. All rights reserved.

No part of this book may be reproduced in any written, electronic, recording, or photocopying without written permission of the publisher or authors.

Published by: *Learn Languages at Home*
Author: Annick Stevenson
with Roger Stevenson, Céline Anthonioz and Vincent Anthonioz
Date of Publication: 2016
ISBN: 978-1-365-07305-2

Main website: www.learnlanguagesathome.net
Others:
—*Learn French at Home*: www.learnfrenchathome.com
—*French Accent Magazine*: www.frenchaccentmagazine.com
—*The French Learning Boutique*: www.frenchlearningmaterial.com
—*Learn English at Home*: www.learningenglishathome.com

Cover photo: Jim Merical.
© Céline Anthonioz

Back cover photo (left to right):
Seated: Roger Stevenson, Annick Stevenson.
Standing: Céline Anthonioz, Vincent Anthonioz.
© Alexandra Anthonioz

A different language is a different vision of life.
Federico Fellini

To learn French is art.
Ben, French artist

CONTENTS

Foreword	Page 13
CHAPTER 1 Jim, the Californian Who Is in Love with France	Page 15
CHAPTER 2 Why Do People Study French?	Page 17
CHAPTER 3 The French Language is Not Such a Daunting Mountain to Climb!	Page 21
CHAPTER 4 Learning is Excellent for the Brain, at Any Age	Page 27
CHAPTER 5 To Learn a New Language Is to Learn a New Culture	Page 35
CHAPTER 6 Speaking French: A Dream That Can Come True	Page 41
CHAPTER 7 Motivation Is a Key to Success	Page 47

CHAPTER 8
Jim's Strong Determination   Page 53

CHAPTER 9
It Is Time to Set Your Goals   Page 57

CHAPTER 10
Don't Just Set Goals. Do Goals   Page 65

CHAPTER 11
Don't Be Fooled by Promises of Instant Fluency   Page 75

CHAPTER 12
Above All: Don't Be Afraid!   Page 81

CHAPTER 13
The Pleasure of Learning Is Another Major Factor Page 89

CHAPTER 14
Find the Right Teacher   Page 95

CHAPTER 15
Studying with *Learn French at Home*:
A Unique Experience   Page 103

CHAPTER 16
Jim's Daily Discipline   Page 113

CHAPTER 17
Listen, Listen, Listen   Page 117

CHAPTER 18
Don't Miss Any Opportunity to Speak   Page 125

CHAPTER 19
Articles, Books, Blogs... Get in the Habit
of Reading in French   Page 135

CHAPTER 20
Write in French... And Have Someone
Correct You   Page 141

CHAPTER 21
Some of the Hurdles You Will Have
to Overcome   Page 147

CHAPTER 22
A Few Hints to Help You Deal with the Main
Difficulties While Speaking with French People   Page 163

CHAPTER 23
When You Start Noticing the Truth About France
By Yourself   Page 173

CHAPTER 24
How to Deal With the Different Phases
of Discouragement   Page 193

CHAPTER 25
Get Ready for Your Trip or Move to France   Page 203

CHAPTER 26
Time to Share Your Knowledge:
French Lessons for Children   Page 219

CHAPTER 27
In Conclusion: Has Becoming Fluent
in French Changed You?   Page 233

ANNEX: A Few Useful Resources   Page 243

ACKNOWLEDGEMENTS   Page 249

REFERENCES   Page 251

FOREWORD

THE MAIN OBJECTIVES OF THIS BOOK are: to motivate those of you who want to learn French — or any other language for that fact —, to encourage you to set goals and to strive to meet them, to help you overcome any obstacle you might encounter along the long road of immersing yourself in a new language, and to fully enjoy the voyage.

This book is the direct result of our experiences as language teachers. We are a team of French teachers giving all our lessons face to face — or, rather, screen to screen through Skype — to individual students of various ages, origins, backgrounds, living all over the world, who all share the same endeavor: learning French, and the same wish: being able to feel comfortable, someday, communicating in this language that they have chosen for whatever personal or professional reason.

From the very beginning and throughout the lessons, we constantly remind our students of the basics of learning any new foreign language, among which the most important might be: "Don't be afraid!..."

Ten years after the creation of our first online school, *Learn French at Home*, followed by the inclusion of other languages, such as *Learn English at Home*, we came to the conclusion that we needed to write a specific self-help book specifically geared to learning French. Such a book does not yet exist.

Learning a language is the introduction to a new land, the land of another culture, which suggests that you should take the time to open the many doors and windows that you will have the wonderful opportunity to meet all along this journey. As the psycholinguist Frank Smith rightly said: "One language sets you in a corridor for life. Two languages open every door along the way." Learning another language may allow you to submerse yourself much more deeply into the culture of another country.

Learn French? Of Course You Can! is a book that will help you to become confident by reminding you that the French language might not be so difficult after all, and that it is rather recent, born from many regional dialects and foreign influences and solidified as a language not too long after the French Revolution. A language that you should not see as a towering mountain almost impossible to climb but as a series of small hills that will allow you, all along the path, to admire its variety, originality, and beauty.

Above all, this book's purpose is to provide you with a multitude of tips and tricks on learning French, and with all the very important self-help advice that we constantly give to our students during their lessons.

Just as our students often become friends over time (friends that we may even invite into our homes after a while), we hope that this book will help you to feel more at home in the French language, to enjoy every minute of your study, to appreciate the progress you make, to have fun, and to not be afraid of making mistakes. After all, the French, too, make mistakes!

Learning a language is an exciting adventure, full of unexpected turns but, above all, it brings a powerful feeling of personal accomplishment and satisfaction.

Alros, prêts pour l'aventure ?

Céline and Vincent Anthonioz,
Annick and Roger Stevenson

1. JIM, THE CALIFORNIAN WHO IS IN LOVE WITH FRANCE

WHAT DO I LOVE about France? Almost everything. I love reading a French newspaper while eating a croissant in the morning at a little sidewalk café, watching people walking in the street, I love Serge Gainsbourg and his provocative attitude, his music, the relationships he had with artists of his generation, I love Juliette Binoche, I love Godard movies, French wines, French cheese, *magret de canard*, the architecture of Paris, especially the Haussmann buildings, the small villages in the South, I love the atmosphere of the *quartier* Saint-Germain in Paris, I love the Seine, the Luxembourg gardens...

We could go on for hours. Jim never tires of speaking about this country that he simply adores, and he loves the French, too, whom he finds "very warm and generous." He also said: "The French language has always held an allure for me, but I don't really understand why." Jim, a typical Californian born in Hollywood, gifted with a very positive and friendly personality, was 15 when he first decided to learn French. But he really started at the age of 45, and then only from a distance, by Skype, first with Céline, the founder of

Learn French at Home, then with other teachers of the same team. He has never been to France more than fives weeks in a row, every two to five years, and still, he has made considerable progress over the years in his fluency in the language. He is now 55, is a busy professional as one can be in the USA, spending long days and evenings solving other people's and companies' computer problems. That is his job. And yet, he has reached an impressive advanced level which allows him to read difficult novels in French, to listen to complex political discussions, to understand the lyrics of many French songs, and to speak easily on the phone with his French friends in their language, or to have interesting conversations with them when they share a dinner together.

Why? Mainly because Jim is, and remains, highly motivated.

There are other reasons, too. As we said, Jim has a positive attitude, he is keen to learn, always remains modest, laughing about his mistakes, and he is never afraid, either to be wrong while saying something in French, or to initiate a French conversation in French with French people whom he does not know. And he has a goal: to be able to walk in the streets, not only of Paris but of any little village in any region of France, anywhere he won't risk meeting people who speak English, and to be able to communicate easily with the locals, to have a coffee and chat with other customers about any news story of interest to them, to live, and speak, like a French person.

Like so many other French learners who try their best to speak and understand better this new language, Jim is doing his best to achieve this goal, so that he can fully appreciate the best of France.

> *...I love Godard movies, French wines, French cheese, magret de canard, the architecture of Paris, especially the Haussmann buildings, the small villages in the South, I love the atmosphere of the quartier Saint-Germain in Paris, I love the Seine, the Luxembourg gardens...*
> Jim, a student of *Learn French at Home*

2. WHY DO PEOPLE STUDY FRENCH?

WHAT IS THE ATTRACTION of France? Why do so many people love this country and want to visit it? Why do they want to learn French?

The French language seems to have become very trendy recently in Anglophone countries, maybe more so than a few years ago. This is evident in many ways. For example, if you add a few words in French to any speech or any presentation of a new play or musical, or if you even slightly alter the script of a musical to add something in French, as we noticed in a few Broadway shows, the public will like it — or at least this is what the producers and performers think. Even Disney movies consider it to be a sign of sophistication. We were surprised when we watched the latest film adaptation of *Cinderella*, to hear an occasional expression in French in the dialogues...

When we ask our students why they want to learn French, they first reply that they want to study the language because France is a country with a rich history and culture. They love the art, beauty and diversity of the countryside, of the cities and of their architecture, and everything else that makes France famous. Overall, they tell us that they particularly like the spirit of independence, luxury products, cheeses, museums (Le Louvre being rated first, with its renewed Italian Mona Lisa), wines, freedom of speech, gastronomy, literature, French cinema, the Eiffel Tower and other monuments, cartoons, croissants, romantic love... And the list goes on and on with everything considered to be the best of France, and that is also very cliché. Even if you point out what is cliché among all this and if you show them other aspects of France, they will keep their rose-colored glasses on and will see France as in Woody Allen's movies, *Magic in the Moonlight* or *Midnight in* Paris, that Jim, and so many other students, adored, of course.

Visiting France is certainly fascinating. But why should anyone learn the language? So many people nowadays travel to Brazil, to Peru, to Thailand, without feeling the need to learn Portuguese, Spanish or Thai. "Because I love this language," most of them say, "especially its intonation," add a few. "Because I love listening to French songs and I want to be able to understand them," others say, or "I want to be able to watch French movies without having to read the subtitles." A few, such as Jim, would even say that they find French politics fascinating and want to know more about it! "I also appreciate the level of political discourse in France and would like to understand it better, especially when I watch *Les Guignols de l'info*", a satirical puppet show on TV that presents a daily interpretation of the news.

However, the majority would say that they intend to visit France regularly because they like the country, and that speaking French would make their trip much more interesting and rewarding; and some may wish to stay a few months in the future, or even buy a house and become an expat... One of our students, R., from Canada, told us that it is the music and lyrics of a French-speaking singer from Belgium, Stromae, who incited him to learn French. Some students have French friends with whom they would love to speak in their language from time to time. Other students would dare to say: "Maybe I will meet a French lover one day if I speak better French?" To which we reply: "Then you shouldn't worry, it is the best way to learn French!" Very few intend to learn French because of a professional necessity, or because they intend to work for a French company or an agency based in France. Much less so than the students of *Learn English at Home*, who, for the majority, have a specific professional goal.

A survey conducted in 2016 of the readers of the magazine we publish every two months since 2006, *French Accent Magazine*, revealed that more than 75% of our readers were learning French out of pleasure, and only 2% for business reasons (the others because they had moved, or were intending to move, to France).

In a rather humorous and provocative editorial, *Do you really want to learn French...? Or...?*, published on the website of the European Parliament, Jean-Louis Boutefeu, a professional French literary translator, started by saying:

> French is a very complicated language, you know — replete with irregular (if not plain illicit) verbs, silent letters, unpronounceable words and exceptions to non-existent rules; an illogical language, periodically attacked by the spelling reformers; a dangerous language, in whose name a misplaced comma can lead to murder and capital letters ceaselessly let slip the dogs of war.

After a few more paragraphs, in which he deplores, among other things, the new habit, partly out of laziness or snobbish taste, that drives the French to use more and more English words in their daily language, he declares:

> Learning French will give you access, in the original, to a whole host of experiences, of which I shall now cite a few pell-mell, with no claims to exhaustiveness: the poems of Baudelaire and Rimbaud, the songs of Nougaro and Barbara, the novels of Camus, Sarraute, Vian, Echenoz and Manchette, the adventures of Astérix and the fortunes and misfortunes of *Le Petit Nicolas*. But, above all, you will gain access to a language which can be gross and subtle at one and the same time — and

tender, moving, elegant, cruel, bitter and icy — a language in which a single sentence, or even a single word, can have ten different meanings depending on intonation alone — a language which has the gift of reproducing the whole gamut of feeling and emotion, human and inhuman, in tones ranging from the hyper-exuberant to the magnificently discreet.

He concludes by saying: "French should be learnt because it is, quite simply, the most beautiful language in all this world and all the neighboring worlds — or, rather, the most beautiful, naturally, except for your own native language."

> *...you will gain access to a language which can be moving, elegant, cruel, bitter and icy [...] a language which has the gift of reproducing the whole gamut of feeling and emotion, human and inhuman, in tones ranging from the hyper-exuberant to the magnificently discreet.*
> Jean-Louis Boutefeu, literary translator

3. THE FRENCH LANGUAGE IS NOT SUCH A DAUNTING MOUNTAIN TO CLIMB!

SOME OF OUR NEW STUDENTS tell us that they are quite intimidated in learning the language of Molière, Voltaire and Rousseau, that they consider to be a very classy and academic language — a very tall and fearsome mountain to climb, at least as challenging as the slope in Albert Camus' *The Myth of Sisyphus*. We emphatically tell these students that it is nothing of the sort. The French language is not an unattainable peak to ascend, but a series of small, charming, green and lovely hills, that are constantly evolving.

French, a rather recent language

In reality, the French language as we know it today is mainly the result of the chaos that preceded and followed the famous French Revolution, which brought to Paris freedom fighters from all the regions — each of them having its own dialect, called *patois*, which severely complicated communication between them. Before the Revolution, 75% of French citizens did not speak French!

It was the period of the Revolution that really marked the transition from a patchwork of dispersed dialects to a more unified and national language. The *révolutionnaires* even led, as an integral part of the revolutionary effort, a war against dialects. This effort was spearheaded by Bertrand Barère (1755–1841), a member of the *Comité de Salut public* (Committee of Public Safety), who was assigned to lead the fight for a national language. In a report "on the idioms" (regional dialects) that he presented before the Convention* on January 27, 1794, he stated his position:

> The monarchy had reasons for clinging to the Tower of Babel. In a democracy, keeping citizens ignorant of the national language, unable to control power, is a betrayal of the mother land... In a free country, the language must be the same for one and all. [...] What money we spent translating the laws of the first two national assemblies into France's various idioms! As though it were up to us to maintain these barbaric dialects and coarse idioms, which now serve only fanatics and counter-revolutionaries!

Since then, the French language has not stopped evolving, continuing to be influenced by the various languages spoken by its very multicultural population. According to the French expert Laurent Chambon, a specialist in minorities, France, compared to other European countries, is by far the most multicultural of all. Very few countries succeeded in bringing together people of origins as diverse as

---

> Before the Revolution, 75% of French citizens did not speak French.

---

* From 1792 to 1795, the first legislative assembly elected by universal suffrage — by male voters only, though.

Africans, Algerians, Armenians, Italians, Russian Jews, Basques, Britons, Corsicans, people from Alsace, the Burgundy or the Poitou region and *pieds noirs***.

Foreign influences

Recently, the French language has been influenced to some extent by an important part of its population, i.e. the people of North African origin, who have even created an amusing and different way of expressing themselves, *le verlan*, which is an inversion of syllables. For example *une meuf*, in verlan, is *une femme* (a woman) pronounced back to front. The *verlan* tendency has been widely adopted by all young French people. With the development of the European Union, the considerable expansion of international exchanges through social media and/or travelling, it is obvious that more and more expressions from foreign languages have found their way into contemporary French, such as German, the Scandinavian languages, Italian, Spanish, Dutch, Japanese and other Asian languages.

Parlez-vous franglais ?

However, it is undoubtedly the English language that has infiltrated the most profoundly the French language, and this as early as the 18th century. It is interesting to note, for example, that words in French containing the letter "w" are all of foreign origin, mainly English. It is also the English language, already very well anchored in contemporary French, which has recently had the most profound influence, especially in Paris and the larger French cities, where *le franglais* has become very common. Indeed, in recent years, the French language has been faced with a new and more profound, although quite peaceful, assault from Anglophone influences that has

---

** French people who lived in Algeria before its independence and came back to France afterwards.

left an indelible mark on how the language is used. The number of English words and expressions used in everyday, modern French is extensive, and one sometimes has the impression that it is necessary to be bilingual to understand what is said or written. In spite of the criticisms among French intellectuals, the Anglo-Saxon wave seems impossible to stop.

As early as 1964, René Etiemble, in his widely published book *Parlez-vous franglais ?*, had tried to criticize the inroads English was making into the French language. At the time, he was quite critical of those who picked up and used such expressions and called for a return to linguistic purity. The French Academy also regularly publishes lists of French equivalents for English expressions that are widely used by the French. The results are always mixed and most speakers of French largely ignore such official edicts and resort to using what everyone else is saying to deal with our changing world. It is really impossible to impose any kind of linguistic norms on a population that is in touch with the rest of the world. In fact, the former minister of culture in François Hollande's Government, Fleur Pellerin, announced in 2015 that "France's resistance to the incursion of English words is harming — rather than preserving — the language." She, in essence, was acknowledging that such efforts are futile and misguided.

The last decade has seen a veritable explosion of English expressions, due largely to the interconnectivity of the entire planet and the generalization of the internet and the associated devices we all use to get online, and one not only has to be nearly bilingual, but also technologically savvy to understand what is going on. *Nerd* and *geek*, not to mention *smartphone* and *ultrabook* (or as one could read in *Le Monde*: *et tous les autres genres de book*), are now accepted expressions. One also hears such things as *overbooké, c'est peanuts, la mémoire flash, un post, un spin doctor, low cost, le feedback, un coach, un pop-up, en live, le tuning, offshore, un hacker, le buzz*, etc. One even sees popular English abbreviations used in text messages such as LOL (laughing out loud), OMG (Oh my God) and WTF (What the f...?)... The French also have a tendency to adopt English expressions and then use them in totally different ways. Some good examples being the word *un lifting* = a face lift, *zapper* = to channel surf, *relooker* = to do a makeover, and *un footing* = a jog, to go jogging.

Could English Become the Future of French?

The list of Anglicisms used in French grows each week, it seems. In spite of the discomfort many traditionalists feel in the face of this unstoppable phenomenon, one cannot deny that the language is made richer and more adaptable by the inclusion of new expressions that better deal with the realities of our modern, interconnected world. "Will French and English at some point in the future become the same language?," Jim asked. "I hope not!," he added.

A French learner of English travelling to Paris will be surprised and amused to hear, and see everywhere in the stores and the newspapers, so many English words. A suggestion: When you don't know the French word or expression when trying to speak to a salesperson or a waiter in a restaurant, use the English one! Either the French person will recognize it and understand you, or he/she will be very happy to learn a new English expression and to add it to his/her vocabulary! Maybe in a few months this new expression will be fully adopted in *franglais*?...

> *The last decade has seen a veritable explosion of English expressions, due largely to the interconnectivity of the entire planet.*

TO REMEMBER FROM CHAPTER 3

• **Don't be afraid of "academic French."** The language in its current form is actually quite recent. It was born with the Revolution, as a more "democratic language," that all the French people could share.

• Before the Revolution, three quarters of French people spoke **only regional dialects.**

• **The French language is constantly evolving.** The last decade has seen a real **invasion of English terms and expressions.**

• **When you don't know the French word** when explaining something to a salesperson or a waiter in a restaurant in France, **try the English one!**

4. LEARNING IS EXCELLENT FOR THE BRAIN, AT ANY AGE

CONTRARY TO A COMMONLY HELD belief, it is possible to learn new things at any age. This is a lesson that the singer Tony Bennett got from "the greatest teacher of music in the world," Pablo Casals. "In our brief conversation about performing music he said: 'At any given moment you can learn.' That sentence changed my life, as it compelled me to never stop learning," Tony Bennett added. There is no age limit for learning. News anchor and columnist Maria Elena Salinas confirmed this assertion with the following anecdote:

> My father, a simple man who was an intellectual, spoke six languages and had a doctorate degree in philosophy. He would walk around with a book at hand at all times. As a little girl, I asked him one day what he was doing, and he replied: 'Studying.' 'Studying at your age?' I asked. He said, 'Of course. You never stop learning.'

Not only does learning improve your knowledge, your understanding, your expertise, your awareness, and, therefore, makes you a more attractive and engaging person, but it has many other crucial benefits: Particularly learning French, or any new language, is well known to be really excellent to improve one's memory, the capacity of one's brain, and even to reduce the risk of contracting Alzheimer's disease. Leonardo Di Vinci was among the first to say: "Learning never exhausts the mind." Nowadays, the confirmation comes from many scientific sources. We don't have the space to detail all of them here and most of them give a very similar assessment. We list just a few examples below.

Learning a language strengthens the brain

A study conducted by four researchers of the Pennsylvania State University, published in the *Journal of Neurolinguistics* in early 2015, concluded that people who learned, with success, a second language, "showed a more coherent and integrated multi-path brain network both before and after training." In an article published already in November 2014 on the University's website, under the title *Learning languages is a workout for brains, both young and old*, one of the scientists, Ping Li, professor of psychology and linguistics, explains further: "Learning and practicing something, for instance a second language, strengthens the brain. Like physical exercise, the more you use specific areas of your brain, the more it grows and gets stronger."

The study was conducted on thirty-nine native English speakers, who were studying Chinese (but Ping Li explains that it would be the same for any language) during a period of six weeks. Before and after the test, all the participants underwent two fMRI scans.

> *Learning never exhausts the mind.*
> Leonardo Di Vinci

While commenting on the results, Professor Li added: "A very interesting finding is that, contrary to previous studies, the brain is much more plastic than we thought. We can still see anatomical changes in the brain [in the elderly], which is very encouraging news for aging. And learning a new language can help lead to more graceful aging."

Like drinking from a mental fountain of youth!...

On a more humoristic tone, but still based on scientifically established facts, William Alexander, a regular contributor to *The York Times* and author of several books, went through a very interesting and surprising experience, which he explains in a book published in July 2014: *Flirting With French. How a Language Charmed Me, Seduced Me & Nearly Broke My Heart*. The main focus of the book is to explain how this 57-year old "lover of France" was disappointed by his poor results when attempting to learn French, which he tried for one year through various schools or systems that we don't necessarily recommend...

However, in parallel to this rather negative experience, he made an amazing discovery. Before he started learning French, he took a cognitive-function exam of his brain, with the intent of repeating it one year later. At that time, he scored below average in his age group for nearly all categories, including ranking in the bottom 10th percentile on the composite memory test and the lowest 5% on the visual memory test.

But when he retook the assessment after one year of studying French, it was a totally different story. "My cognitive scores have skyrocketed," he wrote. For his age group, he placed above average in seven of the ten categories, with his verbal memory leaping to the 88th percentile and his visual memory jumping to the 50th percentile. "Studying French had been like drinking from a mental fountain of youth!" Commenting on his book in a *New York Times* article, he added that spending a year studying French "may have been the best thing I could've done for my 57-year-old brain."

Bilingualism delays risks of dementia and Alzheimer's

An earlier study published in *Neurology* in November 2013, conducted by a panel of nine researchers of the American Academy of Neurology, also concluded that "Bilingualism delays the age at the onset of dementia, independent of education and immigration status." The case records of 648 patients with dementia (391 of them bilingual), diagnosed in a specialist clinic were reviewed. Overall, bilingual patients developed dementia almost 5 years later than those who were monolingual. "A significant difference in age at onset was found across Alzheimer disease dementia as well as front temporal dementia and vascular dementia."

In addition to the above findings, a 2013 research project conducted both at the *Chinese University of Hong Kong* and *Northwestern University*, quoted by William Alexander in a *New York Times* article (*Learning a language as an adult is so hard. That's why it's so good for your brain*), concluded that studying a language is beneficial for older adults because the cognitive tasks involved — inductive reasoning, sound discrimination, memory, and task switching — take place in the areas of the brain most associated with age-related decline.

The more you study, the more your brain gets smarter!

Finally, and maybe one of the most amazing of all the studies published over the last two years, is the one conducted by the neuroscientist Michael Merzenich, Ph.D., a professor emeritus at the University of California, San Francisco. In an article published in *Forbes* in 2013, entitled *How You Can Make Your Brain Smarter Every Day*, he gives the main results of this study:

> The brain is a learning machine, and it needs to be engaged in new learning of different dimensions. The best kinds of exer-

cise are those that challenge. For example [...], seriously undertaking the mastery of a second language is a wonderful thing to do.

It is very interesting to read in more detail the explanation he gives:

> If you're old enough, you may remember a time, maybe back in your childhood, when someone measured your intelligence and assigned a number to it. I suspect that you have been either proud of that 'IQ,' or perhaps a little bit chagrined about it, from that day to this. The general belief back then was that intelligence was a genetic endowment, along with eye color or a propensity for baldness.
>
> We now know this is simply not true. Your brain — every brain — is a work in progress. It is 'plastic.' From the day we're born to the day we die, it continuously revises and remodels, improving or slowly declining, as a function of how we use it.

> *The brain is a learning machine, and it needs to be engaged in new learning of different dimensions. The best kinds of exercise are those that challenge. For example, seriously undertaking the mastery of a second language is a wonderful thing to do.*
> Michael Merzenich, Ph.D., professor emeritus at the University of California, San Francisco

If a brain is exercised properly, anyone can grow intelligence, at any age, and potentially by a lot. Or you can just let your brain idle — and watch it slowly, inexorably, go to seed like a sedentary body.

Most older brains, by the way, are neglected. They are therefore slower and less accurate, and do a poorer job recording useful information and controlling their owners' actions. The common belief, not so many years ago, was that we older folk were just stuck with these declining faculties. Again, we now know this is simply not true. Your brain can be better, stronger, smarter and safer, starting now.

The key is to get 'brain exercise' in the right form. We know that we can sustain or even rejuvenate the brain's accuracy, reliability and problem-solving ability. Most people in midlife and beyond can recover the brain power and adaptive intelligence of those 10, 20 or 30 years younger. [...]

The areas of the brain that control learning and memory require regular exercise. I don't mean just reading new books or acquiring new information through other media. Learning has to be translated into acquiring fundamentally new skills and abilities. We accomplish this by continually developing challenging new avocations and activities. [...] Nothing changes positively in your brain unless it matters to you. Each one of us has the ability to enrich our life and grow our brain power. I strongly encourage you to consider changing your own life, in these and other ways. Take this subject seriously and your brain will thank you!

I wanted to keep my brain active... It works!

We have students of every age, including several older students, who, as soon as they retire, love the fact that they have more time to study French. One of them is Chris, an English civil servant, who told us that he sees his forthcoming retirement as a dream as he will be able to study French seriously, to travel more and to spend more time with his French friends: "I love my French friends, they gave me a lot, they are the best friends I have and I will never forget that." Many students like him confirm that learning French seriously has been like a youth therapy for them! Alan, who has bought a house in the Pyrenees region of France, told us that he wanted to learn French for two reasons: first, "not to be the English idiot" in the village; and, second, "because now that I am retired, I want to keep my brain active. And.. *oh la la*, it works!"

Is it not encouraging to learn that every French lesson or grammar exercise can help you become younger and increase your mental capacities?

TO REMEMBER FROM CHAPTER 4

- Learning is not just for young people.

- The areas of the brain that control learning and memory require regular exercise. Like physical exercise, **the more you use your brain, the more it grows and gets better, stronger, smarter and safer.**

- Nothing changes positively in your brain until **it matters to you.**

- Many studies have confirmed that **learning French**, or any new language, is really **excellent to improve one's memory, one's brain capacities, and even to reduce the risks of dementia and Alzheimer's disease.**

5. TO LEARN A NEW LANGUAGE IS TO LEARN A NEW CULTURE

ONE OF THE MAGIC aspects of learning a new language is that you have the chance to discover a totally new culture. The more you study it, the more you feel the need to immerse yourself in that culture, and to increase your knowledge of it. You will see that this, too, can help improve your brain.

New words, new meanings...

Some cultural differences that appear are readily apparent in the language itself. The same words, even if literally translated, do not necessarily mean the same thing. Pascal Baudry, a French linguist and psychologist, presents in his cyberbook (www.pbaudry.com) some very interesting explanations of intercultural differences between the French and the Americans. He offers this example: With the same word derived from the same verb: "to do" (*faire* in French), you get two different meanings, positive and negative. For the Americans, "a doer" is someone who gets things done, while for the French, *un faiseur* is someone who is arrogant and obnoxious...

In addition, there are so many words that are written exactly the same in English and French but have such a different meaning that it is important for all students of French to learn them and avoid putting themselves in what could be an embarrassing situation. This may be the case among hundreds of false friends with: the verb *blesser*, which means "to injure" and not *bénir* as in English, the word *chair*, meaning "flesh" and not *chaise*, or *coin*, used to talk about a "corner," and not a *pièce de monnaie*. Things become tricky with the adjective *petit*, as *petit coin* is another expression for "toilet," or also the French word *préservatif* which is not at all a "preservative" but a condom!

New words, new feelings

We could also give many more examples of the differences in language that are representative of the differences in culture. What happens is that "speaking different languages means you get different frames, different metaphors, and also you're learning the culture of the language so you get not only different words, but different types of words." This is what George Lakoff, a professor of cognitive science and linguistics at the University of California at Berkeley, said in an article published in *The Atlantic* on October 17, 2014, entitled *For a Better Brain, Learn Another Language*.

In this article, he explains very well how the cultural differences also appear in the feelings you express in each language. Even more,

> *In the new language you are learning, some emotions exist that you cannot feel in your own language simply because there is no corresponding word.*

the fact that, in the new language you are learning, some emotions exist that you cannot feel in your own language simply because there is no corresponding word:

> There are many words that English speakers don't have. Sometimes Anglophones take from other languages, but often, we have to explain our way around a specific feeling or emotion that doesn't have its own word, never quite touching on it exactly. The reason why we borrow words like *savoir faire* from French is because it's not part of the culture [in the United States] and therefore that word did not evolve as part of our language.

Again, learning a new language makes you smarter...

Lakoff continues:

> But the benefits of speaking multiple languages extend past just having access to different words, concepts, metaphors, and frames. Multilingualism has a whole slew of incredible side effects: Multilinguals tend to score better on standardized tests, especially in math, reading, and vocabulary; they are better at remembering lists or sequences, likely from learning grammatical rules and vocabulary; they are more perceptive to their surroundings and therefore better at focusing in on important information while weeding out misleading information (it's no surprise Sherlock Holmes and Hercule Poirot are skilled polyglots). [...] Multilinguals might also be better decision-makers.

Another study done in early 2015 by Lancaster University (UK) has also discovered that a bilingual speaker is better able to entertain different perspectives. "By having another language, you have an alternative vision of the world," the psycholinguist Panos Athanasopoulos said. "You can listen to music from only one speaker, or you can listen in stereo... It's the same with language."

Interesting cultural differences

Apart from the differences in words, grammar, or ways of expressing feelings, when you study French (or any other language), you inevitably learn a lot about all the cultural aspects of the life of a native speaker of that language. Aside from the well-known stereotypes about the French, many specificities of the French way of living or thinking will appear all throughout the learning process.

Among them, and many more that the French learner will be surprised or amused to discover, we can list the following:

—The importance of food for the French, the time spent for dinner with family and/or in the evening, during which they talk very often in depth about their previous, or next, meal.

—The rebellious spirit and political activism of the French, always ready to demonstrate in the streets, to challenge authority, and to avoid, when they can, respecting the law.

—The rather pessimistic or negative way of looking at things that many French share, and *le je m'enfoutisme* (the "I cannot care less" spirit) that they also easily demonstrate.

> *By having another language, you have an alternative vision of the world. You can listen to music from only one speaker, or you can listen in stereo...*
> *It's the same with language.*
> Panos Athanasopoulos, psycholinguist

—The importance of solidarity in a group, i.e. the *associations*, non-profit organizations covering every aspect of life (art, handicrafts, culture, sport, politics, consumer protection, activities for seniors, etc.) that are very powerful and popular in France. One estimates that there are more than 1.1 million such *associations*.

—The many class distinctions in the French society, which comes as a surprise for foreigners. This is indeed another contrast. While the French are said to be very proud of having led the Revolution that supposedly did away with class distinctions, and while socialism with its spirit of equality is a reflection of the thinking of more than fifty percent of the population, France remains a stratified society, in which there are not as many opportunities to bridge the gap between the social classes as there are in the United States, for example.

—The lack of inhibition and prudery of most French as regards the human body is very obvious when you look at French ads or movies. However, by contrast, they demonstrate a very surprising prudery as regards their private life. If you ask a French person you meet for the first time too many direct questions about his/her life or job, he/she can be very offended! Such questions are viewed as an unwelcome intrusion.

A foundation for good discussions

Learning about these cultural differences is really fascinating and makes French lessons much more interesting and fun. During the Skype discussions that all our teachers have with their students, the specificities of French culture are constantly evoked, discussed, and explained, and they are very often the opportunity for a good laugh!

When you have reached a more advanced level, you will invariably be motivated to know even more. One way is to read French literature in French rather than in a translation. Then you will learn a lot, both about the French language and the culture. As George Lakoff said, "there is certainly something to be said for the cultural pleasure of reading Proust's *In Search of Lost Time* in French..."

> ## TO REMEMBER FROM CHAPTER 5
>
> • **Learning new words**, with new meanings, may **trigger new emotions that you have never experienced before.**
>
> • **Multilingualism has many incredible side effects**: Multilinguals **score better** on standardized tests, especially in math, reading, and vocabulary; they are better at remembering lists or sequences and more perceptive to their surroundings, and they might also be **better decision-makers.**
>
> • By having another language, you have **an alternative vision of the world.**
>
> • While studying the French language you **discover many fascinating aspects of the French culture.**

6. SPEAKING FRENCH: A DREAM THAT CAN COME TRUE

ONE OF JIM'S MAIN DREAMS was to be able to understand and speak French easily so that he could immerse himself in a more satisfying and meaningful way into every aspect of this French culture that he finds so fascinating. And now that he has progressed so well in speaking and understanding, he has even started dreaming that, in the future, he will live in France...

Most of our students share the same kind of dreams, starting with the more realistic one: speaking French. It is a true joy to be able to express oneself in another language, to discover a new culture, to enter a new universe which is so different and enticing that it piques one's curiosity... For many students of French, speaking the language and knowing more about French culture is also a dream. A dream that, as is the case with Jim, can become true, even if the path to reach it may seem long and frustrating at times. A dream that requires not only a strong motivation, but a lot of patience and perseverance. But when you have realized it, the rewards are immeasurable.

Once you have acquired a rather good knowledge of French, you will be amazed at the benefits. Not only will you have learned a new way of expression that will immensely expand your universe, but you will be a new person.

"We grow great by dreams," once said Woodrow Wilson, 28th president of the United States, in a very poetic way:

> All big men are dreamers. They see things in the soft haze of a spring day or in the red fire of a long winter's evening. Some of us let great dreams die, but others nourish and protect them, nurse them through bad days till they bring them to the sunshine and light which comes always to those who sincerely hope that their dreams will come true.

Such a strong message can apply to any undertaking, such as learning a new language. In the conclusion to his famous *Walden*, the American author and philosopher Henry David Thoreau gave the same type of encouragement, which, he said, came directly from his own experience: "...if one advances confidently in the direction of his dreams, and endeavors to live the life which he has imagined, he will meet with a success unexpected in common hours."

We could go on with many other quotes by famous persons, whatever their art or specialty. For example, the singer Billy Joel who said: "Follow your dream... If you don't follow your passion, you're not living your life the way you should. As difficult and impossible as the odds may seem, if you're not doing what you love, you're wasting your time." The American author Zhena Muzyka adds an-

> *...if one advances confidently in the direction of his dreams, and endeavors to live the life which he has imagined, he will meet with a success unexpected in common hours.*
> Henry David Thoreau, philosopher and author

other idea that we fully share: "Defining your dreams gives you a destination."

It is only needful for our dreams to be very shiny

Well, French is not a form or art or sport, and you will certainly not have to enter in competition with anyone! Therefore, there is no need that your dream be extremely ambitious. It is most important that it makes you satisfied, proud, happy even. As the writer C. JoyBell C. said in her blog: "It is not needful for our dreams to be very grand nor very big. It is only needful for our dreams to be very shiny." Even if you don't become totally fluent in French, the simple fact that you are able to feel more comfortable in a general conversation when you travel to France, or to get the gist of a French movie without reading the subtitles, will be enough to make you happy.

Having a dream, and setting an objective to fulfill it, is an excellent reason in itself to start French lessons. As you will see later, setting specific goals is very important too, but you must always keep the dream that influenced your decision to take French lessons clearly in mind, even when encountering the normal obstacles and frustrations — such as not progressing as fast as you wished, making the same mistakes over and over again, etc. Dreams are the very basis of motivation, and motivation is a key to success, as we will see in the following chapter.

Are there any good reasons to give up your dreams?

The only impediments that may make you give up your dreams would be:

—**Your own doubts, or lack of** confidence, as the writer Carroll Bryant rightly said in a quote published in her blog: "The only thing standing between you and your dreams is... reluctance."

—**Your fear**. You will see later in this book how important it is to break the fear barrier. The first one you may have to overcome is the fear of telling other people about your dream. In this respect, an interesting anecdote by the TV talk-show host Regis Philbin is related in Katie Couric's book *The Best Advice I Ever Got*. "One of the big mistakes in my mouth was my inability to admit what I wanted to do in my life... But I didn't think I had the talent, so I thought I would sound ridiculous if I even mentioned it to anyone...," he reminds. Then he explains that, during a talk-show, he asked a kid to tell him what his dream was, what he wanted to do in life. The kid was unable to reply. "All of a sudden I saw myself at his age struggling to tell someone what my dream was." Thirty-five years later, at a movie preview in New York, he had the chance to meet the film's director. He was the "kid" who couldn't tell him what his dream was, who had become an adult, and a famous film director: Steven Spielberg! Regis Philbin concludes: "...don't be afraid to dream big and don't be afraid to tell everyone about it. You'll get there faster."

—**Your impatience.** Dreams are not like wishes in fairy tales, they take time to be fulfilled — which can be seen in a positive way: If you realize them too quickly, you are deprived of the pleasure of evolving, of seeing your efforts rewarded, the pride of having overcome the obstacles and obtaining success!

—**Your lack of willingness, perseverance, courage...** which is related to your doubts and lack of confidence. This is partly what this book is about, to help you set your goals and organize yourself in view of avoiding this stumbling block.

You will notice that all the obstacles listed above depend only on your state of mind, and not on your capacities to succeed. Because if you are realistic about what you can achieve, given the available time you have and your own abilities, you will set realistic goals that are adapted to you, or that can be changed according to the way things evolve. Therefore, your personal qualities should not be obstacles that will deter you from meeting your goals.

Another remark, maybe the most important: Don't forget that the simple fact of having the dream of speaking French, of seeing clearly in your mind how things will change for you when you have reached this step, can be an amazing boost for your success. Lailah

Gifty Akita, a very gifted young Ghanaian woman who has several doctorates in science, is the founder of Smart Youth Volunteers Foundation and has written several books on self-motivation, reminds us that "The power of dreams is amazing possibilities."

> *The power of dreams is amazing possibilities.*
> Lailah Gifty Akita, scientist, author and motivator

TO REMEMBER FROM CHAPTER 6

• **Don't forget that your dream of speaking French can definitely come true,** as long as you have a strong motivation, patience and perseverance. **When you have realized it, the rewards are immeasurable.**

• **Dreams are the very basis of motivation, and motivation is key to success.**

• **Set realistic goals** that are adapted to you, or that can be changed according to the way things evolve.

• **The power of dreams is amazing possibilities.**

7. MOTIVATION IS A KEY TO SUCCESS

"I LOVE SPEAKING with the French when I am in France. It seems to me that when one can speak a foreign language one can open a new world," Lucy, one of the students of *Learn French at Home*, said when asked what her motivation was.

> My motivation to learn French is to speak fluently and to be able to write perfectly well essays and letters. [...] Now I am preparing to take the DALF* exam because I need a new challenge. If I succeed, I'll go on to the next step. But from time to time I have the feeling that learning French will be a job until the end of my life.

"To maintain one's motivation can be difficult," another of our students, M., says, even more motivated as he has moved to France two years ago.

---

* DILF, DELF, and DALF are a set of official French proficiency tests; once passed, the students receive an official diploma delivered by the French National Education Board certifying their French competencies at each level.

All our neighbors are French. For us, speaking French is very important. There are always obstacles to overcome. But if we really want to integrate into the society, we have to keep going. We notice that the French are very nice and particularly encouraging when they see you make the effort to communicate with them in their language. Overall, we are enjoying our time in France and we like our life here.

The same need of being motivated when you have a specific objective in learning French is expressed by Alan:

I was a student when I first started to study French, but it was a very long time ago. Thirty years ago, when I bought a house in France, I wished I had been more studious! Therefore, last year, when I retired, I decided that I should take French lessons again. At the beginning, I thought that I would only like to be able to tell my neighbor something easy, such as: 'I'm mowing my lawn.' And then I became addicted. Now I can tell him: 'I mowed it, I will mow it...' - even if I don't have a lawn-mower!

At his age, he added, motivation is not a problem, because "I want my brain to stop giving up."

Highly motivated is also U., who has been learning French for 3-4 months, at the same time as Italian. "I think that the more languages a person knows, the better his chances of succeeding. I have no intention of stopping until I am fluent."

Sometimes, the motivation can simply be to take in the best of a country when one travels.

This is the case for Frank, one of our most faithful students, who lives in Australia, has been studying French for years with *Learn*

French at Home and, almost every year, spends time with a French family in an immersion program:

> I might not use the word 'motivation', but I feel a sort of scar on my self-esteem, which is that I realize I miss so much when travelling in a country if I understand nothing of what the people say. Today one of my motivations is my weekly encounter with my teacher via Skype, and my next immersion, with face-to-face classes, in Montpellier, next September.

Motivation is obviously one of the main criteria when we learn a language and, as we said earlier, motivation is very often born from a dream. We spoke already of Jim's strong motivation, which is really the driving force of all the efforts he has made during the last ten years, and that he continues to make, as he badly wants his dream to come true. He wants to be able to communicate with the French during each of his trips to France. "For me, meeting people, chatting with them, listening to them, is the best part of visiting a country." As long as he cannot speak French as easily and spontaneously as he speaks English, his motivation will remain as strong as it is now.

We can say the same of all our students. During the first interview by Skype with a counselor, not only do we try to assess their level and their specific objectives, but we try to evaluate their degree of

> ...*meeting people, chatting with them, listening to them, is the best part of visiting a country.*
> Jim

motivation. When a person tells us: "I would like to try, but I am not sure if I can make it, if I will be able to learn a new language, I don't really need to speak French so it is not very important for me," etc., we understand that he/she is not very motivated, and we know that it will certainly be more difficult than for someone who is highly motivated. When the person tells us: "I really want to do my best because I need French for such or such reason, I have taken the decision to be able to speak French as I am moving soon to France, I am very motivated..." then we know that our task will be easier.

Without desire, and curiosity, no motivation

If a person is not motivated to study French, it means, above all, that he/she doesn't have a real desire to learn. Without desire, there is no motivation, or at least this is a main lesson we can learn from experience. As the American writer Napoleon Hill once said, "The starting point of all achievement is desire." We could add that curiosity is another good reason to start learning something new, such as a foreign language. Eric Schmidt, the Executive Chairman of Google, goes even further: "Find a way to say yes to things. Say yes to invitations to a new country, say yes to meet new friends, say yes to learn something new... saying yes means that you will do something new, meet someone new, and make a difference." Make a difference? This is another excellent reason to want to try something new.

Of course, there are also more concrete motivations, for example if you are moving to France and understand there is no way you can have a normal life if you don't speak or read French, or when you are hired by a French company to work in their headquarters in Paris. But even if you don't have a pressing need, the desire to learn remains a must to increase your motivation, and your chances of success.

Motivation is something that you have to feel by yourself. Your French teacher can only encourage you, stimulate your desire and motivation by helping you overcome your fear, hesitation, lack of confidence, and increase your knowledge, patiently, at your speed and according to your level and wishes. But your teacher cannot create your own motivation, and your desire, on your behalf.

We do not give French lessons to make a lot of profit from it. We do not look at results by looking at the monthly balance sheet of our bank accounts and ledger sheets. We give French lessons to assist, as much as we can, students who like the language, wish to learn it, and/or need it for any objective, whether it is for work, for vacation, for cultural reasons or because they have fallen in love with a French person. We are just there to help them along the path towards fluency. And teaching a motivated student is much more motivating for us teachers, too!

> *Say yes to invitations to a new country, say yes to meet new friends, say yes to learn something new… saying yes means that you will do something new, meet someone new, and make a difference.*
> Eric Schmidt, Executive Chairman of Google

TO REMEMBER FROM CHAPTER 7

- **Motivation is a principal driving force when learning a new language.**

- **Without desire, there is no motivation.**

- **Curiosity** is another good reason to start learning a foreign language.

- **Motivation is something that you have to feel by yourself.** Your French teacher can only encourage you, stimulate your desire and motivation by helping you overcome your fear, hesitation, lack of confidence, and increase your knowledge.

8. JIM'S STRONG DETERMINATION

SINCE EMBARKING on his intense study of French more than ten years ago, Jim has been determined to succeed. He wanted to speak French fluently on any subject and to make the most of every trip to France each time he had the chance to visit the country. A real challenge for someone living so far from France, who had started from scratch, and had very few opportunities at that time to forge links with French-speaking persons close to his home.

And he succeeded! All the French whom he meets in the USA or during his travels overseas are amazed by his fluency when he speaks French. They are also very surprised by his extensive knowledge of everything related to France. One can talk with him about anything: French literature, movies, music, environment, politics, history or any news story — he is often the first to inform his French friends about what has happened in France during the last hours or the day before. He also has a broad knowledge of many regions of France (Normandy, the Bordeaux region, Provence, the French Riviera, the Champagne region, the Ardèche, the North, the Alps, etc.), knows the differences between the various *quartiers* of Paris and has his personal preferences.

What is the secret of his success? How does he manage to speak French with such spontaneity and fluency, while living in California? Throughout the following chapters, we examine, step by step, how he did it, as well as all the tips and strategies he constantly uses to achieve his goals, and to make his dreams come true.

To start with, the single element that has been the most decisive in achieving such a tremendous success is his strong, constant and unwavering determination. He would never shirk any step of his study, he would never miss a lesson unless he was very sick or overloaded with work, and even if he had to slow down a little from time to time, he would do everything he could to make it up as quickly as possible. Even though he has been taking regular lessons with several different teachers of *Learn French at Home*, he does not think that he has reached the stage where he does not need more lessons.

Furthermore, for some time he started taking a second lesson per week with a French friend who lives close by. "I find all these lessons with my teachers, either by Skype or face to face, very effective, and pleasant. When I have to cancel a lesson because of my schedule, I am always very disappointed. I have the feeling of missing something important." Now, these regular lessons, which consist mainly of a combination of discussions about French culture or politics and a detailed exploration of the vocabulary and interesting expressions, have become a new routine that provides him with great pleasure.

As relaxed and cool as he seems, and he is, his determination has never diminished over the years, on the contrary. He knows what he wants, he has his personal goals, and nothing can deter him from achieving them.

For Jim, as well as for all our students who are the most successful in meeting their goals, determination has been the main factor for such an achievement. As is the case for any discipline. In a quote published on her website, the Indian author and motivating counselor Dr. Roopleen said: "If you have a dream, don't just sit there. Gather courage to believe that you can succeed and leave no stone unturned to make it a reality." For her, determination is the way to make your dreams to come true, as was the case for Jim.

"Desire is the key to motivation, but it's determination and commitment to an unrelenting pursuit of your goal — a commitment to excellence — that will enable you to attain the success you seek," declared the retired Formula 1 champion Mario Andretti.

Just as he made his way through every race circuit he drove in his life, you can make your way along the path of learning you have embarked on, if your determination proves to be strong enough.

> *Desire is the key to motivation, but it's determination and commitment to an unrelenting pursuit of your goal... that will enable you to attain the success you seek.*
> Mario Andretti, Formula 1 champion

TO REMEMBER FROM CHAPTER 8

- The single element that is **the most decisive in achieving success** in learning French is **a strong, constant and unwavering determination.**

- Determination is the essential ingredient for achievement, and the way **to make your dreams come true.**

9. IT IS TIME TO SET YOUR GOALS

SETTING GOALS AND MOTIVATION go hand in hand. As the American writer Robin Sharma says, "selecting goals that engage and motivate you is one of the best ways to boost the level of your personal commitment." He also says: "Setting clearly defined goals provides you with a framework for smarter choices. If you know precisely where you are going, it becomes far easier to select those activities that will get you there." This is, of course, applicable to any choice you make in life. In more general terms, it is interesting to take to heart what Robin Sharma has to say about setting goals, whatever you decide to do and wherever you intend to end up:

> Setting clearly defined goals for all the areas of your life works for three reasons. First, it restores a sense of focus in your world, a world that has become complicated by too many options. In this age we live in, there are simply far too many things to do at any given time. There are too many distractions that compete for our attention. Goals clarify our desires and, in doing so, help us to focus on only those activities that will lead us to what we want.
>
> Setting clearly defined goals provides you with a framework for smarter choices. If you know precisely where you are go-

ing, it becomes far easier to select those activities that will get you there. The second reason that goal-setting works is that it keeps you alert of opportunities. The discipline almost magnetizes your mind to seek out new opportunities... And the third reason why goal-setting works is that clearly defined goals commit you to the course of action. They give you the inspiration to act on your priorities and make things happen in your life rather than waiting for opportunities to land in your lap (which rarely happens). Selecting goals that engage and motivate you is one of the best ways to boost the level of your personal commitment to life and increase the energy you bring to your days.

> *Selecting goals that engage and motivate you is one of the best ways to boost the level of your personal commitment to life and increase the energy you bring to your days.*
> Robin Sharma, writer and motivator

Knowing French is a "must" for many activities in life

Goals are as different as people can be. Some students of French have more concrete goals than others. Getting ready for a job in which it will be important, or a must, to be able to communicate in French with partners or customers, is one of them. Others students may have the goal of taking a French university course, of studying in France or in another French-speaking country, or simply of adding to their resume that they have French as a second, or third language.

It is a fact that knowing at least two languages is always something which will catch the attention of the manager of the company you hope to join, or the interviewer during the job interview.

The simple fact of having been able to learn and, possibly, to master, a second language, may tell more than you think about your personality, your willpower, your courage, your capacity of being open to something else, your curiosity, your originality. Any person working in a human resource department of any company knows that very well.

What learning French can bring to you

Moreover, speaking another language makes you a more accomplished person. This is a fact that all interviewers for any new job are keenly aware of, and that so many famous authors, thinkers, successful leading figures in whatever field have asserted. Here are a few interesting quotes by some of them:

—"Knowledge of languages is the doorway to wisdom." (Roger Bacon, English philosopher, in the 1260's).

—"The limits of my language mean the limits of my world." (Ludwig Wittgenstein, Austrian-British philosopher specialized in the philosophy of mathematics, of mind, and of language, 1922).

—"If we used a different vocabulary or if we spoke a different language, we would perceive a somewhat different world" (Leland

Whitney Crafts, Ralph Wesley Gilbert, Elsa Elizabeth Robinson and Theodore Christian Schneirla, 1950).

Some amusing proverbs, from several countries, also confirm how obvious it is that learning a language can bring so much to an individual. For example, a French proverb says: "A man who knows two languages is worth two men," something that a Turkish proverb confirms in other words: "One who speaks only one language is one person, but one who speaks two languages is two people." But maybe the proverb we prefer is a Chinese one: "Learning is a treasure that will follow its owner everywhere."

A famous Frenchman, the former Emperor Charlemagne, is also said to have added a spiritual thought to such sayings: "To have another language is to possess a second soul..."

So many possible personal goals...

Adding something unique to one's character or personality by learning a new language, in view of using it in one's career, is obvious. However, as we said earlier, we noticed that the majority of those who choose French as a second or third language do not do it for professional reasons, as is frequently the case for English, or do not even think that it might be useful for them in their career. The majority want to study French because they are interested in French culture or they hope to visit the country more often, or because there is something about France, a certain *je ne sais quoi*, that they like, even if they do not always know exactly what it is... Others learn French out of curiosity, of for pleasure, which can be a goal in itself. "I was often able to use my languages, and benefit from them," the amazing linguist and polyglot Steve Kaufmann, founder of *LingQ*, who speaks eleven languages, said. "In learning my languages, I was able to do what the French call *joindre l'utile à l'agréable*, in other words combine usefulness and pleasure."

The objective of learning a language might just be very personal. A person who admires a French actor/actress and is captivated by French movies can set the goal of being able to understand French movies without subtitles. Someone else might simply wish to read French literature in French, or to be able to try French recipes after reading them in the original language, or to have regular exchanges by email or Skype with a French "pen-pal," to enjoy reading French posts on Facebook, to help their children learn another language that might open doors for them in the future, to date a French man or woman... or to go further in the relationship if he/she has fallen in love. To be able to communicate with a person we love in his/her language is a proof of one's deep interest in everything relating to this person. Nelson Mandela had a nice way of explaining how learning another's person language demonstrates how much we care for this person: "If you talk to a man in a language he understands, that goes to his head. If you talk to him in his language, that goes to his heart."

Learning French, or any language, may help you be accepted in a foreign community which will enable you to have a more exciting social life. As Frank Smith also said: "Language is not a genetic gift, it is a social gift. Learning a new language is becoming a member of the club — the community of speakers of that language."

> *If you talk to a man in a language*
> *he understands, that goes to his head.*
> *If you talk to him in his language,*
> *that goes to his heart.*
> Nelson Mandela

An objective for learning French might also simply be wanting to remain young in one's mind, to help one's brain function better, as we stressed in previous chapters. This is the goal that several of our older students have set for themselves, to which they add the pleasure of discovering something new. They are very conscious of what the founder of the American car industry Henry Ford once said: "Anyone who stops learning is old, whether at twenty or eighty."

To go a bit further, studying a language is not only a way to remain young, it is a way to keep your hopes and enthusiasm young. As Lailah Gifty Akita says: "You have to be enthusiastic enough to do what is required for achieving your dreams and goals."

Adapt your goals to your potential and your situation

Now it is time to set your own goals, which can resemble the examples given above, or be totally different. One of the most important pieces of advice we can give you in this respect is to remain modest in your own objectives. For example, it would be unrealistic to set the goal of being totally fluent in three months in view of applying for a challenging job of manager in a French company. If you do so, you are bound to fail. "The person who tries to do everything accomplishes nothing," Robin Sharma says.

Also, do not try to compare yourself to other people you know who have learned French very rapidly and efficiently. Everyone is different, don't even think about getting involved in any kind of competition, which might turn out to be a frustrating experience. "Don't race against others, race against yourself," Sharma adds.

You should not worry, either, about your ego or self-esteem. This is not the point of setting goals, you are willing to learn French in view of a specific result, this should be the only objective.

The American psychiatrist Thomas Szasz, in a text published in 1974, wanted to encourage all learners to think and act as if they were still children: "Every act of conscious learning requires the willingness to suffer an injury to one's self-esteem. That is why young children, before they are aware of their own self-importance, learn so easily."

Setting one's goal requires, therefore, a conscious and sincere reflection of what you intend to achieve, and a realistic view of your own capacities and available time. In this respect, it is very useful to list your goals on paper, to go back to them from time to time to remind yourself what you had planned to do, and to modify them according to the way you are progressing and to the changing constraints that may occur. Any alteration of your goals should, however, be well thought through so that you are not tempted to slowly give up. For some of our students, one of the goals of learning French is only to feel better and more satisfied with themselves. To set such a goal, and go for it, is a first, and very important step, towards achieving it!

> *Studying a language is not only a way to remain young, it is a way to keep your hopes and enthusiasm young.*

TO REMEMBER FROM CHAPTER 9

- **Setting clearly defined goals provides you with a framework for intelligent choices.** If you know precisely where you are going, it becomes far easier to select those activities that will get you there.

- **Knowing French is a "must" for any activity in life**, and can open many doors. More generally, speaking another language makes you **a more accomplished person.**

- **Studying a language** is not only a way **to remain young**, it is a way **to keep your hopes and enthusiasm young.**

- **Remain modest in setting your own objectives.** "The person who tries to do everything accomplishes nothing."

10. DON'T JUST SET GOALS. DO GOALS

THE SAYING FROM the Canadian motivator and leadership expert Robin Sharma, "Don't just set goals. Do goals," may seem obvious. As Napoleon Hill appropriately describes it, "A goal is a dream with a deadline." It is the concrete vision of your deep, and sometimes imprecise, wishes.

Now than you have set your goals about your study of the French language, and that you have a clear picture of what you truly want, you have to make it happen. There would be no need to set specific goals if it were not for following them all along the way, from the day you start studying French, until the day you consider you have finally met your goals.

However, no matter how obvious these sayings are, it is so easy, after a few weeks, months or years, while you are busy with many tasks, professional or family constraints, tight schedules, and hampered by psychological obstacles, to ease up on your concentration so that your goal starts becoming more and more imprecise or too far in the distance, before totally vanishing as New Year's resolutions usually do! Moreover, even if you really want to reach your goal it is very natural to be, from time to time, overcome by tiredness, loss of attention or simply laziness that may prevent you from making the necessary effort, keeping a regular schedule of study and being consistent in working towards the accomplishment of your goals.

To meet your goals: 10 very useful recommendations

Robin Sharma, in his book *Megaliving!*, that we strongly recommend that you read, has examined in depth the phenomenon of setting goals, and offers a very interesting set of recommendations about the best ways of being efficient in view of reaching them. His suggestions can, of course, apply to any type of objective:

1. A well-planned goal will be easier to reach

"Develop a clear plan of how you will achieve the goal and seek out all opportunities for its fruition", he says. "If a goal is too overwhelming," he adds, it will not be tackled and will lead to no result. "But if it is broken down in smaller bits..., it becomes manageable and even fun."

For example, take a French lessons once a week, instead of committing yourself to several times a week, a pace that you may not be able to follow and, at the end, will result in your being discouraged. We know from experience that if you follow a reasonable pace, which allows you to seriously do your homework and learn a few new expressions each time, you progress more rapidly than those who want to learn too fast. "Small victories always lead to large ones," confirms Sharma.

It should be added that for your plan to be effective, it is definitely advisable to start by writing it down, and setting a deadline by which you intend to achieve it.

> *If you follow a reasonable pace, which allows you to seriously do your homework and learn a few new expressions each time, you progress more rapidly than those who want to learn too fast.*

2. Let your goals dominate your thoughts

Robin Sharma gives another very useful piece of advice:

> When one of the world's greatest scientists, Sir Isaac Newton, was asked the key to his awesome success he replied that he thought of nothing else. Study any winner in life and you will see that they have trained their mind to concentrate on nothing but the attainment of their goals. By thinking constantly of the realization of their dreams, they developed a truly unshakable belief and faith that every single one of their desires would come true.

Of course, it has to be adapted to your own situation, activities, and priorities. To concentrate on "nothing but" the attainment of your goal to speak French may certainly be asking too much of someone who already has a busy life and takes French lessons mainly for pleasure or out of interest in French culture! However, the most important idea to retain from this suggestion is: Don't forget your goal, think of it, let in enter your thoughts as something very important you want to achieve, and in doing so you may be more consistent in your efforts, and even learn faster. Moreover, as Sharma rightly says, "Through repetition of thought, the goal will become a burning desire..."

3. Be disciplined — and work as hard as you can...

Let us listen to Robin Sharma, with whom, one more time, we totally agree: "Success in any endeavor requires a focused mind and regular application. Without the power that discipline brings, no dream can be realized." Indeed, following a rather strict discipline will allow you "to shape the tremendously important habit of mind control and positive thinking." He adds that discipline will also "dramatically improve your confidence levels and your productivity as you start to put first things first. Without discipline, or at least a clear desire to build it, you are lost and are destined to be the servant of your mind rather than having your mind serve you."

If you start slacking off, if you start missing too many lessons, if you forget too often to do your homework, your attention may be more easily diverted from your goals towards other activities. In the end, you may simply give up.

Obviously, discipline also means taking your study seriously, and working as hard as you can... "I know the price of success: dedication, hard work, and an unremitting devotion to the things you want to see happen," the American architect Frank Lloyd Wright said. However, working hard on your study of French does not mean, once again, overdoing it! It has to remain within the limits of time and pace that you have established while planning your study of the French language (and that you can always adapt to fit your circumstances, if needed). Getting to the stage of exhaustion, or discouragement, would be as unproductive as not doing enough.

4. Set habits

Erasmus said: "A nail is driven out by another nail; habit is overcome by habit," reminds Robin Sharma, who specifies that "The heart of

> *Success in any endeavor requires a focused mind and regular application. Without the power that discipline brings, no dream can be realized.*
> Robin Sharma

discipline is indeed habit. A habit is like a wire cable. It starts off with a thin thread and through constant conditioning, it becomes stronger and stronger until a time arrives when it cannot be broken."

Our student Jim has developed many habits since he started studying French, such as following a regular schedule of lessons with his teachers, attending discussions on French media followed by a dinner in French every Tuesday evening, taking a few minutes everyday to reply to *La Question du jour* on our French Forum, listening to French podcasts whenever he is driving, etc. Such habits, and others, allow him never to lose track of his study in spite of a very busy professional schedule. We will examine later in more detail how he has organized his study of French.

5. Be confident

We said it already, and we will repeat it again, as it is of a fundamental importance: Be confident, trust yourself, this is a principal key to success. In this regard, Robin Sharma gives his advice in a very interesting way:

> One of the great keys to a better life is to change your self-image. Our self-image is determined by the mental pictures we constantly run through our minds. Our minds work through pictures and when we change the pictures to show what we really want... and what we really can achieve, our self-image will also improve dramatically. This leads to greater confidence and belief in our personal abilities and power. Goals are then easily achieved and the ordinary becomes the extraordinary. Anything you faithfully and honestly believe you can achieve, you will achieve if you take persistent action in that direction. Constantly keep your dreams at the front of your mind. Repeat them all day, every day. Never, let go of them.

6. Be patient

"He that can have patience can have what he will," wrote Benjamin Franklin in 1736. A saying confirmed by, among others, Lailah Gifty Akita, who rightly reminds that you need a lot of patience to keep working. "It takes time for the goals to be realized."

Every French person knows by heart the ending of the fable *The Lion and the Rat* by the French poet and writer Jean de La Fontaine: "Patience and time do more than strength or passion." The famous French playwright and actor Molière, known to be exuberant and trivial but full of wisdom, also said: "The trees that are slow to grow bear the best fruit."

7. Picture your results in your mind

"Picture yourself in your mind's eye as having already achieved the goal, see yourself doing the things you'll be doing when you've reached your goal," the American writer and radio commentator Earl Nightingale said. This should become a habit, also stresses Sharma. Once you have decided on your goal and established your plan that will enable you to achieve it, "picture its attainment in your mind every night just before you sleep. Picture yourself having achieved

> *He that can have patience can have what he will.*
> Benjamin Franklin

your outcome. Make your visualization clear and colorful," he says, reminding constantly that "The magic of visualization can be applied to so many situations" and "can never be overstressed."

As far as you are concerned, you could, for example, visualize yourself visiting Paris, being able to ask for directions, watching a movie and understanding it, reading a French newspaper everyday, ordering a meal in a restaurant where there is no English menu, maybe even chatting with new French friends, etc.

8. Seek support from French friends or acquaintances

"Get as much support behind you as possible," suggests Robin Sharma. Having a support network will keep you focused, motivated and inspired. This can be any organized group of Francophiles close to where you live, forums on internet, or simply French friends who have expressed the willingness to help you and with whom you can be in regular contact, through social media or regular gatherings.

This is exactly what Jim does; he doesn't miss a chance to attend any French event in Southern California, and he has a solid team of French friends close to his home with whom he meets very regularly. We will come back to this later, with our advice on the type of support you can obtain.

9. Have fun

We will also come back to this very important aspect in a full chapter of the book, but it should already figure in your goal making. "Have fun and reward yourself," Sharma says, quoting the sages of the East:

> Enjoy the journey. [...] Treat yourself when you achieve even the smallest of your goals. Small victories bring large victories. And do not be too hard on yourself if you don't achieve a goal on schedule. Be flexible. Try another approach but never, ever

give up if your aim is worthy. [...] Happiness comes from achieving goals...

10. When needed, review and reassess your goals

We mentioned earlier that as important as it is to draw up feasible plans, it is crucial to adapt them to any change that may occur in your life, or to your availability and possibilities. "Once you take the time to set and regularly review your goals, your mind will spot opportunities to allow your desires to be fulfilled," Robin Sharma concludes.

> *The magic of visualization [...] can never be overstressed.*
> Robin Sharma

TO REMEMBER FROM CHAPTER 10

- **A well-planned goal is easier to achieve.**

- **Don't forget your goal, think of it**, let it enter your thoughts as **something very important you want to achieve**, and in doing so you may be more consistent in your efforts, and learn faster.

- **Be disciplined, and establish habits.**

- **Be confident, trust yourself, and be patient.**

- **Picture the results in your mind.**

- **Seek support from French** friends or acquaintances.

- **Have fun!**

- When needed, **reassess your goals.**

11. DON'T BE FOOLED BY PROMISES OF INSTANT FLUENCY

"WE WANT FAST FOOD, fast service and fast learning. But some things do take time, disciplined effort and hard work," explains Robin Sharma.

We can only fully agree, and add that fast learning is as tasteless as fast food, and that if you want to appreciate fully what you are learning, you definitely need time. You need time to learn, in any case. Don't believe in the misleading slogans used by some schools promising that you will learn French in thirty days, or that you can be totally fluent in three months. This is nonsense.

Of course, if you make a real effort and work intensely, you can get the basics of easy communication rather quickly, but what you will have learned will remain on the surface, and you will be very frustrated when you visit the country if you can hardly read a restaurant menu, or do your best to say a few words that nobody understands. One of our students, C., told us about his frustrating experience, after having studied French for less than one year.

> When I went to Morocco for meetings with people from a Ministry, I was expecting that they would take place in English (such arrogance!) but I realized quickly that my counterparts spoke only French. Therefore, I survived with my

'schoolboy French' but it was not pretty! Then I decided to make the effort to study more seriously.

As we noted in the previous chapter, having patience and taking your time while learning is fundamental if you want to be able to fully understand, memorize, and make real progress towards speaking fluently. You will learn much easier and in a more natural way than trying to hurry things along and not paying attention to many important aspects of the French language. If you subscribe to a "fast learning program," you may not get sufficient exposure to French grammar and the more interesting idiomatic expressions. Without a basic understanding of grammatical principles, you will never be able to speak proper French. This is why, in the various programs provided by *Learn French at Home*, we register beginning students only in "Regular program," which includes teaching of grammar and homework, as it would be useless to limit the lessons to conversation sessions or even our intensive program, as none of them is appropriate for beginners.

Wanting to learn too fast can bring frustration and anger

If you subscribe to a school program that promises you that you will speak French in three months, even if you work intensively and with devotion, when you try to talk with anyone in France you will realize that you are not really communicating but simply speaking for the pleasure of listening to your voice. For example, trying to buy *métro* tickets at the booth of the subway during rush hour, or any other little undertaking of the sort, might very well turn into a traumatic experience, leading to a mutual lack of comprehension or even anger. We have heard so many similar stories from people who did not want, or could not find the time, to study French in the proper way, that we are always very frank with our new students: Forget learning very quickly and, on the contrary, devote your available time and energy to walk at your own pace along the path to better knowledge, not forgetting to appreciate fully at each step what you have already learned or discovered about the French language and culture, and to take as much pleasure as possible in this adventure. For the students who study in this way, everything they finally master after working on it for a while is like a real victory, and an immense source of satisfaction.

So, how long will it take me to speak French?

We are constantly asked this question, which is one of the most difficult to answer. It all depends on so many factors — your level when you start (if you have studied a little already at school), your ability to learn a new language, your capacity of memorization, the difficulties you may have (or not) with the pronunciation, the time you can devote to your lessons, the type of lessons you choose to take, the homework you can do and your own discipline in doing it, etc. — that there is not a single, pat answer to that question.

It all depends, as well, on what "to speak French" means for you. If you mean understanding enough not to get lost when travelling, being able to ask for directions or checking-in at a hotel, or even exchanging a few words with French people, then you may easily be able to acquire in a few months what we call "survival French." Some students tell us that they were able to make real progress — express themselves better, even if still slowly, understand better the news on TV and radio — in only ten months. But most of the time you will need much more than that, especially if you want to reach an advanced level. There are so many French idioms used in everyday language that you will not be able to have a real conversation with a French person without understanding at least a few of them. Verb conjugations present another difficulty, and the pronunciation is often a real challenge. Usually, we would say that you may need between one to two years to reach an intermediate level, and more to become totally fluent. Some of our students have done very well in three years, others are still struggling after five years of study, depending of their available time and other factors mentioned above. If you only spend between one to three hours a week on French lessons or any other self-teaching technique, then you may need a few years. Jim started studying French more than ten years ago and now he is almost fluent, but he still has a lot to learn, which he likes, as he takes the whole process of learning in the most positive way. To discover new idiomatic expressions, for example, is a real joy for him and helps him understand better the typical French way of looking at things and the French *joie de vivre*.

If you intend to take the series of DELF-DALF exams, and if you devote considerable time to this study, you may need up to one year to advance from one level to the next. This is why, unless you have a specific professional objective, we would advise you not to impose extremely strict deadlines on yourself for becoming fluent in French. Instead, it may be excellent, as suggested in the previous chapters, to set realistic goals for every step of your learning progress. Each time you reach the level you wanted to attain, it will be very rewarding. Then, you can set the next goal, and just go on, at the same pace if possible, along the road to discovering this language, a process which, as we have already said, will also improve your knowledge of the French culture and will enrich you in so many ways.

> *Fast learning is as tasteless as fast food.*

TO REMEMBER FROM CHAPTER 11

- **Don't believe in the misleading slogans** used by some schools promising that you will learn French in thirty days, or that you can be totally fluent in three months. This is nonsense.

- **If you want to appreciate fully what you are learning, and take pleasure in it, you definitely need time.**

- **Be patient, take your time**, this is the way to learn with more ease and in a more natural way than trying to hurry things along and not paying attention to many important aspects of the French language.

- **You may need between one to two years** to reach an intermediate level, and **more to become totally fluent.**

12. ABOVE ALL: DON'T BE AFRAID!

BREAKING THE FEAR BARRIER that you inevitably encounter when you learn a new language is fundamental if you want to progress. We cannot stress this very important aspect too much. Be brave, courageous, open, and don't be shy if you do not feel comfortable speaking French in the very beginning, and you will soon notice that the pressure this fear is exerting on you will lessen. Breaking the fear barrier, and doing it repeatedly each time you feel afraid again, is a necessary step when learning a new language — a new anything, actually, whether it is a sport, an art, a handicraft, a technical skill, a profession, etc. As the Brazilian novelist Paulo Coelho asserts quite strongly: "There is only one thing that makes a dream impossible to achieve: the fear of failure." Fear "can also stop you for from doing creative or exciting or experimental things," actress Helen Mirren said.

Stanley Kubrick relates these feelings to education in general: "I think the big mistake in schools is trying to teach children anything, and by using fear as the basic motivation. Fear of getting failing grades, fear of not staying with your class, etc. Interest can produce learning on a scale compared to fear as a nuclear explosion to a firecracker."

This remark is very applicable to adult education, as well, and to any type of study. Our experience has taught us that our students who study French with passion or personal motivation are more successful than those who are hampered or restricted by the fear of not being able to succeed.

As we explained earlier, the French language is not a high mountain to climb, but a language that constantly changes, and in which more and more foreign words, especially those from English, are integrated, which makes it easier for English-speaking learners. This is yet another good reason not to be afraid to begin studying it!

Gain self-confidence

Nobody but you can have a complete understanding of why you have decided to study French, of your goals, objectives and personal interests. Nobody should be able, or have any reason, to discourage you from following the learning path that you have mapped out for yourself. Therefore, we suggest that you avoid seeking advice, comments or recommendations, unless it is from someone who fully understands what you are doing and who shares the same enthusiasm for the French language, someone you trust and who can really help you, such as a member of the network of friends and French people we suggested that you establish. By doing so, by just continuing your study, at a comfortable pace, you don't have any reason not to be totally self-confident, or to fear the judgment of anyone else.

As much as you can, try to remain cool, and feel as secure as you can, following Beyoncé's intelligent advice: "Have patience. Have grace. Be secure enough in yourself to base success on personal growth."

Don't be ashamed to talk

Another type of fear is that of feeling ashamed to speak broken French to people you don't know. This is another barrier you will have to break in your learning process and you will feel much better when you have succeeded. The only solution is not to hesitate to speak in French any time you may have the opportunity, without worrying about what others will think of you. Many of our students told us how afraid they were when they started their French lessons, such as Helen, who lives in the Picardie region in France: "After living in rural France for 18 months and realizing that my school French just wasn't going to miraculously come flooding back to me (without some assistance!), I decided to take the plunge and contact *Learn French at Home.*" She told us how she was "dreading" speaking French from a distance, without having her teacher face to face.

However, my fears were totally unfounded as Céline turned out to be an absolute star! She is so kind, patient, considerate and encouraging. It never fails to amaze me how positive and upbeat she remains, especially when you keep making the same old mistakes week after week and you just feel like it's never going to sink in. Each new grammatical point is carefully explained and utilized in varying contexts, so that there's no possibility of misunderstanding. I genuinely feel after 5 months of lessons that I am finally making progress and I am no longer bothered about making or taking those scary phone calls. For any of you who are still not motivated, they've re-

> *I think that the big mistake in schools is trying to teach children anything, and by using fear as the basic motivation. Fear of getting failing grades, fear of not staying with your class, etc. Interest can produce learning on a scale compared to fear as a nuclear explosion to a firecracker.*
> **Stanley Kubrick**

cently discovered that learning a foreign language greatly decreases the risk of your getting Alzheimer's, so, as a lady of a certain age myself, I'd say, 'Let's go for it!'

Your teacher is not the only person who will be patient with you when you try speaking French with him/her. You will see that, most of the time, the French persons with whom you make this effort will respond positively, and be ready to help you. We will revisit in depth later in the book the importance of speaking and of not being shy about doing so.

At the beginning, you may feel like a child again

Part of the pleasure of studying is that, when you start learning a new language, or anything else, you feel a little like a child again — even if the process of learning for an adult is very different. At the beginning, your knowledge of the French language will be similar to what a toddler is able to say. At each stage of your progress, you will advance to the level of knowledge of a little child, then to that of a teenager, then to that of a young adult... "A foreigner born in a foreign country... has, in general, not even the level of a 1st grade child. Therefore, I have to advance humbly, little by little, even if I scarcely have the level of a small schoolboy, or of a preschool child... I must learn like a child," wrote Arimasa Mori, a Japanese writer, philosopher and translator who spent most of his life in France, quoted by Akira Mizubayashi.

You are, of course, not a child anymore, and you will not actually revert to this period of your life, but you will certainly, from time to time, have this feeling. This is totally natural, there is nothing to be embarrassed about, as some people may feel. On the contrary, you just have to acknowledge it, and make the best of it — including the fun of discovering, playing with words, laughing at the bizarre cultural differences in ways of expressing things that you will encounter during the whole process. Also, the idea of learning like a child should help you to be more relaxed, less concerned by the image you will have of yourself and of your ego. As we said before, young children are not yet aware of their self-esteem. The polyglot Matthew Youlden goes further: "To be seen failing (or merely struggling) is a social taboo that doesn't burden children. When it comes to learning a language, admitting that you don't know everything (and being okay with that) is the key to growth and freedom. Let go of your grown-up inhibitions!"

"At the beginning, I felt like a child," Jim told us frequently. "I was reading some children's books in French and I couldn't even understand everything." However, instead of complaining, he accepted the situation and it added to his motivation to learn more and to reach a higher level of knowledge. Many of our students have made the same type of remark, and most of them acknowledged that there is something enjoyable about feeling like a child again for some time! In the book selection of our magazine *French Accent*, we sometimes recommend children's books in French as a way to access a certain part of French culture and literature, and to enhance your vocabulary. We even publish an easy poem or nursery rhyme as part of our pedagogical material. Looking at the world around you with the eyes of a child can teach you a lot.

Accept the idea that you will make mistakes

"We learn by making mistakes," Matthew Youlden adds. "As kids, we are expected to make mistakes, but as adults mistakes become taboo." Yet, absolutely every individual who goes through the process of learning, in whatever field or art, knows exactly what it is to make mistakes, and has to accept it, deal with it, and learn from it.

Jim knows that very well too. However, he understood long ago that he could not avoid saying something bizarre from time to time, and he has the intelligence to turn it into a funny and memorable experience.

Asked if he were afraid of making more errors while speaking with French people, he replied: "Of course I am afraid! But the fear I have today is not so much to make a fool of myself but that I will say something insulting." Jim now knows, from experience, that this is part of his charm for the French people he meets. But he remains very careful: "I definitely don't want to shock the nice people with whom I talk!" Jim also knows very well that when you have said something really funny, this is an excellent way to learn not to make this mistake again, and that there is really nothing to be too ashamed of. This is part of the learning process, and it can only help you to progress.

As Robin Sharma says, there is "nothing wrong with making a mistake." And he adds:

> You are a human being and human beings have been designed to make mistakes. As long as you don't keep making the same errors and have the good judgment to let your past serve you, you will be on the right track. Accept them and move on... Coming to the realization that we all make mistakes and that they are essential to our growth and progress is liberating. [...] This is a powerful way we all learn and grow.

Don't be afraid to make mistakes, and to have the feeling of looking stupid from time to time. The American actress Lisa Kudrow confirms, with wisdom: "I've learned you can make a mistake and the whole world doesn't end. I had to learn to allow myself to make a mistake without becoming defensive and unforgiving." While a Chinese proverb has an amusing way of advising you not to be afraid of being ridiculous when you ask for something in a silly way: "He who asks may be a fool for five minutes. He who doesn't ask is a fool for a lifetime."

And you will see later in the book that more and more French people make a lot of mistakes in their own language, too...!

Don't be too hard on yourself

This is another important recommendation that we could recall. Some students are too hard on themselves when they have the feeling that they are not making as much progress as they would like. Most of the time this feeling does not correspond to reality. Even if you think that you are not progressing, this is not always the case. You never stop learning, memorizing, enriching your vocabulary. A recommendation to other French learners given by one of our students, Shelley Ruddock, from the UK, who moved to France is: "A foreign language and a country's culture cannot be learnt overnight, so don't be too hard on yourself."

Finally, do not forget that learning a language is a personal commitment. It is very similar to yoga in this respect, and also given the fact that your own pace is very personal. You should never, ever, try to compare your progress to that made by other students. More importantly, make the best of it, and enjoy the process!

> *I've learned you can make a mistake and the whole world doesn't end.*
> Lisa Kudrow, actress

TO REMEMBER FROM CHAPTER 12

- **Breaking the fear barrier** that you inevitably encounter when you learn a new language is **fundamental**.

- **Be brave, courageous, open, and don't be shy** if you do not feel comfortable speaking French in the very beginning, and you will soon notice that the pressure this fear is exerting on you will lessen.

- **Gain self-confidence**, avoid seeking too much advice.

- **Don't be ashamed to talk.**

- **At the beginning, you may feel like a child again.**

- **Accept the idea that, like everybody, you will make mistakes — and don't be too hard on yourself!**

13. THE PLEASURE OF LEARNING IS ANOTHER MAJOR FACTOR

WHEN YOU LISTEN to Jim, what stands out is the real pleasure he derives from being able to speak French, and also from continuing to learn the language. "Since my first lesson with Céline, more than ten years ago, learning French was terrific! I just loved it. These one-on-one lessons are very effective, and so pleasant!" He likes everything, even those things that many students do out of necessity but not by passion, such as studying grammar or writing in French.

> I love writing essays as part of my homework. I adore replying in French to the *Question du Jour* of the Forum... I love listening to French broadcasts and podcasts and to French songs. I take so much pleasure from reading books in French, even when they are very difficult and when I need my teacher to help me understand a few paragraphs.

Many of our students have similar experiences, and we receive a lot of positive comments from them telling us that they are not only satisfied with their progress, but that they really enjoy studying the language. For example, a student in the UK, Mata, wrote: "Just to tell you how much I have enjoyed the lessons (never thought I'd say that about learning another language!)." A. Mohan, who lives in Charlottetown Canada, also said: "The lessons are lots of fun and the time flies by." Another student, Toni O'Sullivan, in Ireland — who is a teacher herself and ended up giving English lessons for us when we created *Learn English at Home* — wrote to us: "The course is absolutely brilliant and totally enjoyable... each week has been a pleasure." Sevahn, who lives in Detroit (USA) and who had a *coup de foudre* (love at first sight) for the French language, is also very enthusiastic: "I enjoy immensely my French lessons.... It is a very unique and delightful way to learn how to speak one of the most beautiful and romantic languages in the world!..."

We could go on and on quoting students who make the same kind of statement, that we would not necessarily expect from students in a school. "I am learning very well," "I make good progress," "My results are very satisfying," would be the kind of positive reactions that we would normally expect from them. Most of the comments we get underline the fact that the pleasure of learning is at least equally important as the material learned. "Each lesson is a wonderful experience, a real joyful moment," Jim insists.

Pleasure and good progress go hand in hand

Robin Sharma regularly gives this advice to his readers: "Learn to associate a tremendous amount of pleasure with learning. You will never be disappointed and your life will become one inspiring adventure." He also likes to say: "Enjoy the journey towards your goals.

> Each lesson is a wonderful experience,
> a real joyful moment.
> Jim

Have fun and be playful." The German mathematician Carl Friedrich Gauss even says: "It is not knowledge, but the act of learning, not possession, but the act of getting there which grants the greatest enjoyment."

This is very true. This aspect of the learning process is fundamental. If you do not take any pleasure in it, you miss one of the nicest aspects of learning, and you may even reduce your chances of succeeding. It is the same, in fact, for any kind of endeavor. Ina Garten, the Bestselling cookbook and television host, once said: "If you love doing it, you'll be very good at it." Beyoncé insists also on the importance of seeing everything one is doing with a positive spirit: "Choose to be happy and positive…"

The comments made by our students to the effect that, even without thinking of it, they find happiness and fun in their lessons, are among the most encouraging kinds of feedback that we receive. For them, it is a guarantee that they will learn with much less difficulty. As we have noticed so often, pleasure and good progress go hand in hand, and we would even say that without pleasure, you will not go very far.

Keeping a sense of humor

Equally important is to keep one's sense of humor. Laughing is one of the best ways to release tension.

Most of our students noticed that when they can laugh with their teacher about something that they find very difficult to understand, or ridiculous, in the French language (and it happens very often), this helps them a lot to memorize what they have laughed about. One of our students, Peter, who lives in Northants, UK, recently wrote to us about the weekly sessions he has with Céline:

> I have found her method of teaching excellent in that she encourages you to make progress whilst at the same time ensuring that mistakes are corrected without any element of de-

motivation. I consider this to be important because the way we progress in many areas of learning is by making mistakes and learning from them. The lessons are very enjoyable and we laugh a lot about the oddities of each other's language and the different ways in which language is used... I'm certainly enjoying the experience.

During many of our lessons, we also like teaching our students a few jokes about strange French habits or some of the difficulties of the French language, such as this humorous remark from the American actor Steve Martin, quoted in *The New York Times*, that we particularly like: "Boy, those French! They have a different word for everything." And we regularly publish on our Facebook page very funny short videos on learning French and good French jokes. We consider these examples of humor an important element of any pedagogical material!

> *Boy, those French! They have a different word for everything.*
> Steve Martin, actor

TO REMEMBER FROM CHAPTER 13

- Most students get **a lot of pleasure** from studying the language and find it **fun**.

- **Pleasure and good progress** should go hand in hand.

- Don't forget to always **keep your sense of humor. Laughing** is one of the best ways **to release tension**.

14. FIND THE RIGHT TEACHER

AS JIM SAYS REPEATEDLY, it is essential to have a teacher, even if you intend to work a lot on your own while learning French.

> For me, my French lessons are indispensable. It is very important to have real conversations with a good teacher. It is great to listen to French radio or to do anything possible to improve one's understanding, but it is equally important to be able to express oneself in real time. For that, conversations with my teacher are very effective.

Of course, nowadays there is a multitude of very well-done websites from which you can learn, listen to French pronunciation, do auto-corrected and fun exercises on every aspect of the grammar and test and improve your vocabulary. Most of them are excellent tools, and we strongly recommend that you take advantage of them as a very useful complement to your study. They provide important follow-up practice, they enable you to consolidate what you have learned and to obtain further explanations, to get the right meaning of certain words or expressions and to translate them, to reassure you that you have made good progress, or simply to have fun while playing word games. But this is not enough. You need to have someone who can accompany you during this fascinating journey of learning a language, someone who will be your guide while you are progressing towards your personal goal. Someone who can explain to you the nuances of the French language and provide you with some essential insights into the culture, who will discuss in French with you and correct you gently when you make a mistake or will help you improve your pronunciation, who will give you specific and appropriate homework, and correct it, and who will give you feedback, and escort you at each step along the way.

However, when we say that a teacher is indispensable, we mean a "good" teacher.

What is a good teacher?

There are many definitions of a "good" or of the "best teacher," with which we fully agree. For example, for the American politician Brad Henry, "A good teacher can inspire hope, ignite the imagination, and instill a love of learning." "Good teachers know how to bring out the best in students," the American journalist of CBS Evening News Charles Kuralt adds. We also agree with the other former anchorman of CBS, Dan Rather, when he says: "The dream begins with a teacher who believes in you, who tugs and pushes and leads you to the next plateau, sometimes poking you with a sharp stick called 'truth'." And, of course, we would be remiss not to include Albert Einstein who said so rightly: "It is the supreme art of the teacher to awaken joy in creative expression and knowledge."

> *It is the supreme art of the teacher to awaken joy in creative expression and knowledge.*
> Albert Einstein

While all of this is true, we would add something which we find fundamental: A good teacher is someone who, at first, is willing to get to know you, to listen to you, who pays a lot of attention to you and who is truly interested in who you are, what you like, what you intend or hope to do, someone who cares about you. Second, a good teacher is someone who is able to adapts his/her way of teaching to your style, your personality, your interests, your wishes, so that he/she is sure to help you in the best way possible.

Therefore, a good teacher is someone with whom you have, beginning with the first lesson, shared your dreams and your goals — who may even have helped you to set your goals if, at the time, you have felt unsecure or uncertain —, and who does his/her best to help you to achieve them. A good teacher sees you as a unique person, has consideration and respect for you, does not, under any circumstance, judge or criticize you. He/she understands you, is positive, is able to reassure you, gives you intelligent and useful feedback and does not allow you to get discouraged. A good teacher is someone with whom you always feel comfortable, at ease, even if he/she pushes you to your limits, with whom you are able to share your thoughts, with whom you have fun and thoroughly enjoy each lesson, with whom you may even share a love of the French language, as Jim does with his French teachers. He adds that, for him, a good teacher is not only someone who teaches something and builds on his abilities, but also someone who encourages him to think and question.

One of our favorite definitions of what a teacher should be can be found in the wonderful book *Tuesdays with Morrie* where the author, Mitch Albom, writes: "Have you ever really had a teacher? One who saw you as a raw but precious thing, a jewel that, with wisdom, could be polished to a proud shine? If you are lucky enough to find your way to such teachers, you will always find your way back." Because for your teacher, you have to be someone special, as William W. Purkey, the American writer, professor of counselor education in North Carolina, and co-founder of The International Alliance for Invitational Education, also rightly explains:

A Student is the most important person ever in this school... in person, on the telephone, or by mail. A Student is not dependent on us... we are dependent on the Student. A Student is not an interruption of our work.. the Student is the purpose of it. We are not doing a favor by serving the Student... the Student is doing us a favor by giving us the opportunity to do so. A Student is a person who brings us his or her desire to learn. It is our job to handle each Student in a manner which is beneficial to the Student and ourselves.

> *A good teacher is someone who is willing to get to know you, to listen to you, who pays a lot of attention to you and who is truly interested in who you are, what you like, what you intend or hope to do, someone who cares about you.*

What kind of learner are you?

Figuring out how you learn is an important aspect of successful language learning. If the teacher teaches in a way that does not suit your style of learning, you might lose interest in the lesson and give up the idea of learning French altogether, which would be a real shame.

Many students are not quite sure what stimulates them until they have started their French learning experience. Perhaps you enjoy best learning through games? Or you enjoy trying to express yourself through casual conversations? Or perhaps you need to get a lot of feed-back in order to gain confidence in speaking? Or you are the type of person who needs to know the ins and outs of the language and all of your questions must be answered before you move on? Perhaps you need to write everything down in order to be able to memorize the new information? Some people enjoy the challenge of understanding the fine points of grammar while others are put off by it. Certain students work best through repetition and others need a lot of visual aids. The best way to find out your style of learning is by taking private lessons. A good teacher should be able to understand what stimulates you, your pace of learning, and which method works best for you. It might take a few lessons but eventually he/she should be able to plan a lesson which works for you. If not, then do not hesitate to tell the teacher what appeals to you the most, and if he/she doesn't show any flexibility in his/her lesson plan to suit your style of learning, then we would suggest that you try with another teacher. Being able to personalize the lessons to your objectives, motivations and pace of learning is what makes a good teacher. The lesson experience should feel comfortable and at the same time be stimulating.

Beware of teaching that is too "academic"

This is why we do not consider that teaching French, or any other language, should be done in a too academic way. Instead, it should be done in a very personalized and positive way, so that the student gets the maximum out of his/her lessons, and makes real progress. There are many schools for adults all over the world with teachers who are able to teach in this way.

Unfortunately, there are also many French teachers who have been influenced by the rather rigid French education system, which means: following a pre-formatted program, or book, without too much personalization or feedback, and sometimes not much encouragement — if any at all. Not all French teachers in the academic system (either in France or French studies programs all over the world) are so strict, far from it. This does, unfortunately, happen, and you will rapidly be aware of it.

One of the major problems with academic teaching is that you may not learn common everyday French, the "real" French that French people speak. During an interview with James and Elma Durrand, a British couple who settled in the western part of France, they told us: "Not long after we came to Parthenay, a local shopkeeper said that although we were learning French at a local college we would still have to learn how to talk French in the French way! How right he was! I think we will be learning for many years to come!"

We would advise you to try to find your good teacher by reading online forums, listening to word of mouth recommendations, and by not paying too much attention to pretentious and glossy advertisements from schools with a reputation that may not always be justified.

We hope that, whomever you find, he/she will be a "good" teacher. If not, you may wish to find someone else... This is why we offer you one more piece of advice: Do not commit yourself for too many lessons or for a full program before first having had the experience of a few lessons, i.e. before knowing your teacher better and being sure that you feel completely comfortable with him/her.

> *One of the major problems with academic teaching is that you may not learn common everyday French, the "real" French that French people speak.*

TO REMEMBER FROM CHAPTER 14

- **It is essential to have a teacher**, even if you intend to work a lot on your own while learning French.

- **A good teacher will be your guide** while you are progressing towards your personal goal. Someone who can explain to you the nuances of the French language and provide you with some essential insights into the culture.

- **Beware of teaching that is too "academic."**

- **A good teacher sees you as a unique person**, has consideration and respect for you, does not judge or criticize you. He/she understands you, is positive, is able to reassure you, gives you intelligent and useful feedback and does not allow you to get discouraged.

- **Do not commit yourself for too many lessons** or for a full program **before knowing your teacher better** and being sure that you feel completely comfortable with him/her.

15. STUDYING WITH *LEARN FRENCH AT HOME*: A UNIQUE EXPERIENCE

"CORINNE IS SIMPLY THE BEST teacher I have ever had! I have no idea how she can be so patient with me and always so encouraging," wrote Sarah Sapper, one of our students in London. "The lessons are always varied and she is always suggesting different things for me to read or listen to. I can't believe I am saying it, but I actively look forward to Monday evening when I have my lesson." An example of many positive comments from our students about their French teachers.

It is now time to introduce to you our language school, how it works, our experience with teaching with distance learning technology, but while you are comfy at home. When Céline and Vincent Anthonioz started *Learn French at Home*, in 2004, there were almost no schools offering personalized one-on-one lessons on Skype with a teacher who is sincerely interested in you and who follows your progress over time. The need for such distance schooling was obvious, as so many people who want to learn French find it difficult, most of the time because of their heavy professional schedules, to attend regular lessons in a school or any other institution. Also, depending on where one lives, it is often difficult to find good language schools, or independent French teachers, very close by. There are some people, too, who cannot very easily leave home to attend classroom lessons, such as mothers with young babies, older students, or children already very busy with their school schedule. The hours of the lessons offered by language institutions are also not always convenient for people who work late and who are available only in the evening or during the weekends. And there are also people who travel a lot and would appreciate being able to continue studying from a hotel room or any other location during their trips.

Learn French at Home can meet all these needs, thanks to the use of Skype, and also to the flexibility of our teachers, all French native speakers and very good professionals who are located all over the world and who can easily adapt their schedule to those of our students, wherever they live. This is a major asset of the school.

Another advantage is that we make every effort to insure that all our teachers are pleasant and considerate, and that they provide a positive and encouraging learning experience and remain devoted to their students, as the examples in the previous chapter so clearly illustrate.

Since its creation, more than 3,000 students have placed their trust in our French courses. Today, we have students who live in France, Canada, the UK, the USA, Switzerland, Germany, Belgium, Holland, Brazil, Latvia, Australia, Japan, Liberia, Singapore, China, Russia, the Philippines, etc. All of them can confirm that *Learn French at Home* is a serious, caring, and reputable language school, and they appreciate the personalization and the continuous feed-back which accompanies the lessons, as well as the kindness, and flexibility, of the teachers.

> *Today, we have students who live in France, Canada, the UK, the USA, Switzerland, Germany, Belgium, Holland, Brazil, Latvia, Australia, Japan, Liberia, Singapore, China, Russia, the Philippines, etc.*

Flexibility is a must for the majority of students

Bonnie Priest, who lives in the UK, told us:

> Carine is a terrific teacher; just the right mix of encouragement, patience and instruction. The format really suits me, as well. I like being able to take the lesson at home (or when I'm travelling) and at a time that suits me. Carine, although busy, is very good about finding a time each day for a lesson. I also really like the ability to have a Saturday lesson — the one day of the week that I'm not thinking about a million other things. Overall, I am extremely happy with the lessons.

Flexibility is definitely a real advantage for the majority of our students, and also the fact that the teaching is always adapted to their needs. "I found my lessons extremely worthwhile," Ian, in Basingstoke, UK, said. "Vincent is an excellent teacher, he tailored the lessons to my specific requirements of leading a group of tourists and readily revisited aspects that I did not initially understand."

"I like the flexibility of learning this way because I can have weekly lessons regardless of where I am in the world," also confirmed Paul, who resides in the Dordogne region of France. "I am also learning French quicker than with other methods or lessons because it is easier for me to schedule them."

> *I like the flexibility of learning this way because I can have weekly lessons regardless of where I am in the world.*
> Paul, a student of *Learn French at Home*

A teacher who cares

"My life changed when I found *Learn French At Home*," our British student Sarah Rundle said in replying to a questionnaire. "I feel so much more confident now. The teachers have endless patience, even when you make the same mistake over and over again. The lessons are fun, totally non intimidating and structured in a way that you work hard in an enjoyable way. Above all you can laugh."

Apart from flexibility, our students are very appreciative of the kindness and attention of their teachers. "I have been studying French off and on for several years," wrote Sandy Parker (Florida, USA) who has several members of her family living in France — but when she visits them, they insist that she speaks English with her three grandchildren so that they remain perfectly bilingual.

> I've taken several classes at a University, I've hired private tutors, I've taken classes with *Alliance Française* and *Berlitz* and have tried teaching myself with various books and CDs... Of all the ways I have tried to practice and learn the language, your method has been the best and most impressive. I was skeptical to try it, but... I can honestly say this is the best course/class/method I have encountered.

She further adds that her teacher "is an exceptionally gifted teacher, she sets a good pace, she explains things well, she encourages me to expand my knowledge, she challenges me and she manages to do all that in a charming and creative manner!"

Another English-speaking student, Robby Collins, in Lausanne, Switzerland, similarly expresses his satisfaction with his teacher:

> You should know that I am very picky when deciding to recommend someone. I am extremely happy with Audrey, and

the courses over Skype. It has helped me so much and I can see improvement almost daily. In fact, I am progressing much faster than some of my colleagues who are in face-to-face group lessons.

His comments are confirmed by A. Mohan:

> I have studied French with several teachers, but find *Learn French at Home* to be the best in terms of quality and value for money. In the past, I had found that not every school, (including those that are rather expensive) is able to effectively teach French. My experience, however, with *Learn French at Home* has been very positive. M. Benjamin is an excellent teacher. I am impressed with how unique and personalized the teaching methods are, particularly the scenarios which force me to speak French outside the basic conversational topics that I am very familiar with. The lessons are also lots of fun and the time flies by. The combination of homework, weekly lessons and the daily questions on the *Learn French at Home* website mean that I study French and use what I learn everyday.

Teachers with diverse backgrounds

There are various programs, according to the needs and level of the student, but the most popular are the "Regular program" and the "Conversation sessions," and some students also appreciate being able to take "A la carte" lessons, which are even more adapted to their needs. In such cases it is very important for the student to have a teacher who knows quite well his field of activity, and the jargon used in it. In addition to our highly qualified and experience teachers, many of them have professional experience in a wide variety of fields.

For example, a student who is a writer and needs some help to prepare TV interviews in France to talk about a book that has just been translated into French will be assigned a teacher who is a former journalist who will know what kind of questions this student may face. A United Nations official who has to prepare conferences on development in Africa will feel much more confident if his/her teacher has experience working for the UN and is knowledgeable about development issues.

The same is true for an artist who wants to prepare for an exhibit, a scientist who has a lecture to give to a French audience, an athlete who will compete in a French-speaking country, etc.

All of the above are just a few examples of lessons that have already been given and which proved successful. Individuals who already speak some French and who need to prepare very quickly for a special event also have the option of choosing an "Intensive course" which runs for five consecutive days (one hour per day). This option has also proven quite effective.

How do the lessons take place

In all cases, the teacher and student communicate by Skype. Each lesson, which lasts from 30 to 60 minutes and consists mainly of an oral exchange, is designed to improve the student's general speaking abilities and listening comprehension. First, the teacher and student chat a little about anything they wish. Then the lesson will include a conversation, and/or different role plays, exercises, games, and questioning. The objective is to have the student feel comfortable by the end of the lesson with the new information he or she has gained. The teacher gently corrects the pronunciation and the little mistakes made by the student.

After the lesson, the student receives by email the teacher's notes from the Skype chat board, together with another text or article to study and, for the "Regular" lessons, some homework (a written assignment and/or some grammar to study and exercises to do) that the student sends back by email to the teacher before the following lesson and that the teacher corrects and returns.

Comfortable and enjoyable lessons

Strangely enough, this semi-anonymity helps many students to feel more relaxed and less self-conscious. "I love that!," one of our English students, Helen, told us.

> I think the fact that I don't need to worry about my appearance, the way I am dressed — sometimes when I have lessons on Sunday or early in the morning I am still wearing my pajamas! — helps me to be very comfortable, not to be intimidated by my teacher, and finally to learn better. Learning from home is such a great idea! This is what I call freedom.

Other students have even been so bold as to tell us after a few lessons that while they are speaking with their teacher by Skype in the evening, they are drinking a beer or a glass of wine... Another way to relax and to really feel like they are entertaining a friend at home.

> *I think the fact that I don't need to worry about my appearance, the way I am dressed, helps me to be very comfortable, not to be intimidated by my teacher, and finally to learn better. Learning from home is such a great idea! This is what I call freedom.*
> Helen, a student of *Learn French at Home*

Feeling totally comfortable is also the feeling expressed by Toni O'Sullivan:

> My teacher is wonderful. We get on so well and we talk about anything and everything, all the while I am putting my spoken French to the test and at the same time learning, as Audrey is writing up any queries or corrections, yet never stopping the flow of conversation. Audrey always has the answers to my (MANY) questions and has a great way of explaining. She always makes the homework personal to me, so that it is relevant to my needs. I find Audrey to be warm, interesting and patient, we laugh a lot together and she is very motivated and encouraging...

Toni adds that she is "amazed how quickly you progress and how much fun you have in doing so."

Most of the programs are offered in packages of 4, 8, 12, 22 and 35 lessons (the cost decreases according to the number of lessons). There is never any obligation to choose a long series of lessons, and we always advise our students to start with no more than four lessons so that they can see if the study is suitable for them, and if they like their teacher.

When your teacher becomes a friend...

The lessons always take place in a relaxed and friendly atmosphere, but it also happens after some time that your teacher will become a real friend. Maybe it is because you learn from home, and your teacher is also giving the lesson from his/her home and not from a school or an office, or because you speak together without seeing one another, or because you cannot have a lesson without chatting a little about personal matters, there inevitably comes a time where you get to know one another very well and care for one another... At any rate, we discovered after a few years of experience that your teacher may very well become your confident, and a very good friend!

This is something that, obviously, is a great help for the student to memorize and to improve his/her knowledge of the French language. Each lesson becomes a privileged moment, such as a rendez-vous with someone you are very happy to meet. "It has become a pleasant habit to talk once a week with my tutor, the lessons are very fun and we chat non-stop, there are many jokes and laughs," Frank wrote on our Forum. "For me, it is like a cocktail evening, I drink a glass of wine and we jump from pillar to post, especially me." It is the same for Jim, who is one of our best friends now, and with several other American, English, Japanese, Australian students... All the founders of the school, as well as several teachers, have established links with some of their students which extend far beyond the French lessons — and last even beyond the time when the student is actively taking lessons.

> *It has become a pleasant habit to talk once a week with my tutor, the lessons are very funny and we chat non stop, there are many jokes and laughs. For me, it is like a cocktail evening, I drink a glass of wine and we jump from pillar to post...*
> **Frank, a student of** *Learn French at Home*

TO REMEMBER FROM CHAPTER 15

- **There is a real need for distance schooling,** as **so many people who want to learn French find it difficult**, most of the time because of their heavy professional schedules, **to attend regular lessons in a school** or any other institution.

- Since the creation of *Learn French at Home*, **more than 3,000 students, all over the world**, have placed their trust in our French learning courses.

- **Among the major assets of our school**: The **teachers** are **totally flexible**, and **really care** for their students.

- All the lessons, mixing conversation, role plays and homework, **are adapted to the needs, the level and the personality of the student.**

- **No long-term commitment is required.**

- **Not only the students make very good progress but they find their lessons comfortable and enjoyable.**

- For some students, **their teacher even becomes a friend** after some time...

16. JIM'S DAILY DISCIPLINE

JIM WOULD NEVER DREAM of missing any opportunity to listen to, speak or read French. Apart from his professional commitments, French accompanies him all the time, and this has been the case for a very long time. When *Learn French at Home* started an online Forum in 2007, giving the students the opportunity to answer the *Question du Jour* on any subject of life (and to be corrected online by the teacher who posted the question), he was among the first to sign up, and over the years, he has almost always submitted his answer to the daily question. From 2012 to 2015 alone, he has written more than 1,500 posts, the wide majority of which express his love for France, or relate frankly and with humor some of the difficulties he faces on a daily basis in his study of the French language.

Participating in the Forum is part of the daily discipline Jim has established for himself. First, during breakfast, he reads a few pages of a French publication, such as *France*, a magazine specializing in French culture and *joie de vivre* to which he has subscribed. Then, using his computer or iPhone, he opens the webpage of the *Learn French at Home* Forum, reads the corrections by a French teacher of his previous answers and the answers of other students, discovers the new daily question and the first answers, and writes his own in French. Then, he is ready to go to work and gets in his car. As a computer consultant, he spends a lot of time driving, going from one client to the other. For him, this is the best time to listen to the French podcasts he has previously downloaded: French radio programs or recorded French lessons. He alternates with French songs or French news. In the evening, before going to bed, Jim reads a few pages of a French novel, in the original language. His discipline includes a few other activities several times a week. At least one morning a week, he has a French lesson, by Skype, with a French native teacher based in France; and every Tuesday evening, he has another lesson face-to-face with a teacher and friend who lives close by — a lesson which ends with a dinner with a few French friends during which the rule is: to speak only French. On weekends, when he has more time, Jim loves watching French movies and, when subtitles are available, he prefers the subtitles in French. He also enjoys spending some more time over an aperitif or a dinner with French friends. And even when he is gardening, on Saturday morning, he listens to French podcasts on his iPhone.

"Success is created through the performance of a few small daily disciplines that stack up over time to produce achievements," Robin Sharma says. Jim's advice to any student of French is to follow as much as possible the same type of discipline that he has applied for himself for more than ten years now: "I know from experience how much listening to French radio is good for the comprehension." He adds that it is very important to learn the grammar. "If you don't understand how to put a phrase together or how to conjugate the verbs properly, you are lost. You may understand what French people around you are talking about but you are unable to participate in the discussion."

Jim is an excellent example of what many of our students try to do in order to make sure they are on a right path for learning: discipline themselves within a daily or weekly routine. One of them, Lindsay, who lives in France, listed in the Forum all of the New Year's resolution that she intended to keep:

> to continue reading French newspapers every morning; to read at least one French magazine each month (I receive two of

them: *Vent Sud* and *Détours*); to answer the *Question du jour* of the French Forum of *Learn French at Home* at least three times a week, if I like the question; to speak regularly to my neighbors, to attend each of my cooking classes which take place twice a month in my village; to attend a French-English conversation group every Friday; to do all the homework that my teacher gives me.

As we said in the chapters about goals, drawing such a specific list of tasks is an excellent way to discipline oneself, and not to forget any useful step on the pathway towards a better knowledge of the language.

> *Success is created through the performance of a few small daily disciplines that stack up over time to produce achievements.*
> Robin Sharma

TO REMEMBER FROM CHAPTER 16

- **Establish a daily or weekly routine for yourself.** Learning with a teacher, as indispensable as it is, is not sufficient. **Try to find many other ways to practice your French**, such as reading a newspaper, listening, meeting French people, etc.

- **Drawing up a specific list of tasks** is an excellent way to discipline yourself.

17. LISTEN, LISTEN, LISTEN

AMONG THE LESSONS we can draw from Jim's experience is the importance of listening to French in order to progress. He now understands much better any dialogue, his vocabulary has been enriched, and he is much more comfortable and confident in speaking the language.

Whatever you intend to do in life, whatever you are interested in, to be able to listen carefully, in view of understanding and memorizing, is excellent. "I like to listen. I have learned a great deal from listening carefully. Most people never listen," once said Ernest Hemingway." Steven Spielberg had the same experience: "From a very

> *I like to listen. I have learned a great deal from listening carefully. Most people never listen.*
> **Ernest Hemingway**

young age, my parents taught me the most important lesson of my whole life: They taught me how to listen... When you listen, you learn. You absorb like a sponge."

Especially when you learn a language, to be able to listen, and to do it as often and regularly as possible, is a fundamental aspect of the learning process. It is an indispensable exercise if you want to get accustomed gradually to the pronunciation, as well as picking up new vocabulary and ways of expressing ideas or opinions.

Learn to listen to your teacher

It stands to reason: Listening to your French teacher seems obvious. However, it happens quite often that, when you are face-to-face with your teacher, or in a class with a group of students of various levels, you do not fully understand everything that the teacher is saying because you focus more on his/her attitude, the context of the explanation he/she gives, or the reaction of the other students. One of our English students, Kathy, living in the Cognac area in France, stressed the importance of "learning to listen to the spoken French word." She explained that the *Learn French at Home* method of teaching by Skype, with the webcam off, i.e. without seeing the face of her teacher, gave her a unique experience: This "has helped me to train my ear to listen instead of just trying to get by with guessing what is being said from the speaker's gestures and intimations." Paul, also living in France, confirms: "I have to listen and concentrate more because there is no body language to see, but this is improving my ability to pick up the sound of words... Even my 9 year old son has commented how my French is improving and he is fluent!"

However, even if you listen carefully to your teacher during each French lesson, this can never be enough. If you want to learn French, you have to avail yourself of as many opportunities as possible to listen to spoken French and work on your listening comprehension. All students should take full advantage of the many resources available on the internet. Below are a few suggestions.

Watch films, listen to the radio or podcasts...

Anything is worth listening to: news, sports events, ads, weather forecasts, game shows, short funny sketches, travel or literary programs, any good websites with audio links... This can be done almost anywhere and at anytime. For example, Robin Sharma strongly encourages listening to audio recordings in the car while commuting. "Turning your car into a 'college on wheels' will be one of the best investments you will ever make," he says. The same applies if you take the train, a plane, a metro, a bus, when you have no one to talk with. This is one of the main benefits of any type of smartphone or other device, you can take advantage of any "lost" time while travelling to listen to French.

We also recommend that you regularly watch French films (preferably with subtitles in French instead of in your own language). Not only will that give you the chance to practice your listening comprehension but you will also be able to see and hear people speaking French between themselves. If you do not live in France and do not have access to French films, you can certainly rent DVDs or download movies through any streaming service.

Jim has many suggestions for listening material that he includes in his daily discipline, and you will find them in the Annex at the end of this book. Most of our students use similar ways to listen to French when they can, and they confirm that it helps them immensely, such as Lindsay who told us, through our Forum, that she subscribes to the French channel *Canal+* and watches regularly

> *Anything is worth listening to: news, sports events, ads, weather forecasts, game shows, short funny sketches, travel or literary programs.*

French news and from time to time a French movie. "I also listen to the French radio through the internet and in my car, and every week I try to do a few comprehension exercises through RFI (*Radio France Internationale*) on the Internet. Slowly, but little by little, my understanding is improving!" "I fully agree that watching French TV and listening to French radio is very important for my study of French," confirmed an American student, Ren.

A French film is also a perfect window to many aspects of French culture. Even if it is only "cinema," and obviously often exaggerated or contrived, it can give you a good picture of how the French react when faced with various situations and the way they express their feelings.

Listening to songs is also a wonderful exercise

It is almost the same with songs. It is well known that listening to songs is a good tool when learning a language. The rhythm, as well as the emotions expressed, help you memorize the words, the voice of the singer also can be catchy, and listening to a French song is another way of learning more vocabulary, especially everyday expressions or idioms used by the singers. Moreover, it tells you more than you may think about French culture.

Many French students are reluctant, at first, to try listening to French songs, saying "I don't understand a word." But it is so easy nowadays to listen to a song on YouTube while reading the lyrics that you can readily find on one of several websites (see Annex). If you can connect with someone (a French friend, or their teacher) who can explain to you the meaning of each line, you may very well end up loving such an exercise.

Jim has become a fan of French songs. At the beginning, he used to listen mainly to Francis Cabrel and Serge Gainsbourg but he has quickly expanded his knowledge of the French music scene, and we could even say that he has become a sort of specialist as his repertoire is as wide, if not wider, than that of many French people! This is impressive.

Jim, who is also a musician, is obviously even more sensitive to the music and the poetry of the songs, but he also has fun trying to figure out the many plays on words contained in the songs — something that French singers are particularly good at!

Indeed, one of the characteristics of French songs is, as we call it in French, that they are *des chansons à texte*, meaning ballads in which the lyrics play a major part, sometimes even more than the music itself. Many of these songs are also protest songs, or songs with a message which touches the listeners and that frequently has a certain influence on the French people, and even on political figures. Such aspects are very interesting for a student who wants to immerse himself/herself more into French culture.

Below is a good example of a typical *chanson à texte*, by the very popular French composer, songwriter and singer Jean-Jacques Goldman, who is actively involved in many humanitarian causes. This song speaks about three characters who practice different professions: a shoemaker, a teacher and a musician. All of them, in their own way, have helped change the life of other people for the best, or at least have brought something positive to them:

Il changeait la vie

C'était un cordonnier, sans rien de particulier
Dans un village dont le nom m'a échappé
Il faisait des souliers si jolis, si légers
Que nos vies semblaient un peu moins lourdes à porter

Il y mettait du temps, du talent et du cœur
Ainsi passait sa vie au milieu de nos heures
Et loin des beaux discours, des grandes théories
À sa tâche chaque jour, on pouvait dire de lui
Il changeait la vie

C'était un professeur, un simple professeur
Qui pensait que savoir était un grand trésor

Que tous les moins que rien n'avaient pour s'en sortir
Que l'école et le droit qu'a chacun de s'instruire

Il y mettait du temps, du talent et du cœur
Ainsi passait sa vie au milieu de nos heures
Et loin des beaux discours, des grandes théories
À sa tâche chaque jour, on pouvait dire de lui
Il changeait la vie

C'était un petit bonhomme, rien qu'un tout petit bonhomme
Malhabile et rêveur, un peu loupé en somme
Se croyait inutile, banni des autres hommes
Il pleurait sur son saxophone

Il y mit tant de temps, de larmes et de douleur
Les rêves de sa vie, les prisons de son cœur
Et loin des beaux discours, des grandes théories
Inspiré jour après jour de son souffle et de ses cris
Il changeait la vie...

Translation :
He Changed Life

He was a shoemaker, with nothing in particular that set him apart
In a village whose name eludes me
He made such lovely shoes, so light
That our lives seemed a little less heavy a burden

He put his time, talent and heart into it
And thus he spent his life among us
And far from great speeches, from great theories
He went about his task each day, one could say of him
He changed life

He was a professor, a simple professor
Who thought knowledge was a great treasure
And that was all the nobodies had to make do
And that school where everyone has the right to an education

He put his time, talent and heart into it
And thus he spent his life among us
And far from great speeches, from great theories
He went about his task each day, one could say of him
He changed life

He was a little man, nothing more than a wee little man
Clumsy and a daydreamer, a bit botched in a way
He felt he was useless and cast out by other men
He cried on his saxophone

He put his time, tears and pain into it
The dreams of his life, the prisons of his heart
And far from great speeches, from great theories
Inspired day after day by his breath and his cries

> *He was a professor, a simple professor*
> *Who thought knowledge was a great treasure...*
> Jean-Jacques Goldman, composer, songwriter and singer

TO REMEMBER FROM CHAPTER 17

- When you listen, you learn.

- **Learn to listen carefully to your teacher. Learning through Skype without a webcam**, as *Learn French at Home* students do, **is an excellent way to "listen to the spoken French word," without any body language** that might help to understand what your teacher is saying.

- **Watch films, listen to the radio or podcasts and to songs.** All of this is extremely useful to get used to the spoken French language.

18. DON'T MISS ANY OPPORTUNITY TO SPEAK

ANOTHER LESSON we can draw from Jim's experience is that you should not miss any opportunity to speak French with French natives, either in France, of course, during your trips, but also anywhere in the world when you have the chance to meet French speaking people. The first thing to have in mind is not to be afraid to do so! We talked earlier of the very natural and humane fears you encounter during your study of French, and particularly of your fear of making mistakes, and of feeling like a fool if you make mistakes when talking to French people, either in person or on the phone. If you want to speak properly — and it will never be enough to do so only with your teacher — it is essential that you gain confidence in yourself.

Sometimes, we agree, it is easier said than done. "Each time I find myself in a situation where I should say something to a French person whom I have just met, I have the feeling that I have forgotten everything I have learned and I am unable to say a single sentence that makes sense," one of our students told us. This fact of having the feeling of losing your memory when you are in a situation of stress is well-known. Shannon Hale, an American writer of fantasy books, puts it this way in the mouth of one of her characters in *The Goose Girl*: "Clearly she was expected to say something, but panic at having to speak stole the thoughts from her head." You are even more stressed if someone from your family or a friend, assuming that you will be happy to speak French with someone you encounter together, tells you: "Why don't you speak French together? Go ahead, say something!" Such a situation may quite often be very embarrassing...

Practice with your teacher

The first thing is to gain confidence by practicing as much as you can, and the first person with whom you will do that is your teacher. It is not enough to exchange a few words and then work on a specific text which you will already be familiar with. It is very important that you engage in "real life" conversations, especially before you travel to France, and if you know that you may have the opportunity to meet some French people. During the lessons given by the teachers of *Learn French at Home*, we always try to help our students get ready by creating some role plays adapted to the situation they may encounter. We also make sure that the students know very well how to introduce themselves and are familiar with the customary expressions used by the French when they meet someone for the first time. Such conversational formulas are also reproduced in our e-books and we encourage our students to listen to them and to repeat them over and over again.

The more you feel confident speaking naturally with your teacher, the easier it will be to do the same with other French natives. In order to help you improve your speaking skills, your French teacher will encourage you to dialogue a lot with him/her.

> *The more you feel confident speaking naturally with your teacher, the easier it will be to do the same with other French natives.*

Some of our students are originally from countries where the study of a foreign language privileges the written skills. This is the case for example in many language schools in Japan. When we have such students, it is, therefore, all the more important to focus mainly on speaking the language.

The French will react very positively

When you think you are ready, it will be time to take the plunge and start trying out your speaking skills with French people! For that, you have to keep in mind what we have already said: Most people with whom you dare to take the first step and begin a conversation with, will react very positively and be ready to help.

This is why you should not hesitate to talk to French people that you may encounter during your trips to France, or people you have the opportunity to meet in your country. You will be surprised how positively responsive they can be. They are not going to judge you negatively because you are speaking French to them; most probably, they will be pleasantly surprised, will find you courageous and perhaps they might even be a bit amused. Either way, you will gain respect and admiration from them.

When speaking to French natives, do not hesitate to ask them if what you said was correct, if you have used the right word, or even the right verb conjugation, and to ask them how you should have expressed what you wanted to say.

Perhaps, you're thinking: I might annoy the French if I ask them to help me or if I try to speak with my limited French! It may bother them, of course, if you insist a bit too much, or if the conversation you are trying to have lasts a bit too long. But you should be able to appreciate the limits of their patience. Generally, the French are grateful that you are trying to speak their language.

You should also not worry at all about annoying, insulting or embarrassing anyone: If you start your conversations by saying *Mon français n'est pas très bon, je suis désolé(e)* (My French is not so good, I am sorry), then you've warned the people with whom you intend to exchange a few words, and you should feel more confident in speaking. For example, even if you have learned the correct usage of the *vous* and the *tu* forms — and if you know very well that if you want to be respectful, it is always preferable to start with *vous* with people you do not know — you may be totally confused when you meet people and possibly forget all this, and say *tu* spontaneously. That is perfectly OK, the person with whom you are talking will certainly not be offended and may just find it amusing.

The French are very tolerant when these often unspoken rules are broken by foreigners — you are allowed to make mistakes — and if you think, each time you are not sure of what you are saying, or if you realize you made a blunder or said something not appropriate, just add expressions such as *pardon, je suis désolé(e), excusez-moi* (various ways to say: I am sorry, excuse me), *s'il vous plaît* (please), *merci beaucoup* (thanks a lot), etc. And, of course, you should also never forget to say *bonjour* and *au revoir* (good bye). We will come back to that later.

Shelley Ruddock told us once:

> All the people I have spoken to have appreciated the fact that I have made the effort to speak French, and when I say to them, 'Pardon for my poor French', they always say, 'Please don't apologize, because I can understand you!' Generally, I always try things out even if I think I cannot quite remember the sentence perfectly, because after I have said it once I can always go back and improve it for the next time! [...]
>
> The main thing is confidence, and being able to remind myself of all those high moments when at times you begin to feel a little frustrated. Learning a language isn't easy. We have to remind ourselves that people do look at you with admiration and that most people won't learn another language.

Don't be ashamed of your accent!

It is a well-known fact we often consider foreign accents appealing and charming. On the other hand, we hate listening to our own accent when we try expressing ourselves in a foreign language! You will be surprised to realize that the French really like your accent when you speak French to them, whether you are English, American, Australian. etc. This fact has been confirmed by a study published in May 2015 in the weekly *Connexion*: "French people consider the English accent to be the most attractive — while the rest of the world considers the French language to be the most seductive." This was the result of a poll of 14,000 people worldwide who use the language learning application Babbel. "For the French people who were surveyed, the language of love was Italian and the most attractive accent to hear someone speaking French was the English one, taking 39% of the vote."

Even if this has not much to do with accents, the study also reveals that "nearly 95% of respondents worldwide said they would be ready to learn a new language for a relationship..."

> *French people consider the English accent to be the most attractive — while the rest of the world considers the French language to be the most seductive...*

while in France, talk with salespersons

To create as many opportunities as possible to speak French, let the salespeople speak to you! If you live in France, you will most definitely receive a few phone calls on a weekly basis from a company trying to sell a product.

One of our French students made us laugh when she told us: "I love it when a salesman calls me! I see it as an opportunity to learn

French!" She was right... The salespeople want to sell; therefore, they will more likely be patient and pleasant over the phone. And if you don't live in France and simply travel in the country, it may be the same with many salespeople that you meet in stores — especially if they feel that you might be a good customer!...

This is what Jim does each time he travels to France: He loves going into any shop, whether a cheese shop or a clothing store, and chatting with the salespeople there. With all the charm that a Californian has for a French person, Jim manages to develop excellent relations with some of them. Asked what his favorite store is, he replies:

> The first thing that comes to my mind is my preferred *fromagerie* in Paris. It is an immense pleasure for me to go there. Of course, there is a very good selection of cheeses, and the shop owner can explain to me the specialty and all of the subtle aspects of each piece of cheese. When I go there, I always ask for her advice, depending on my desire of the moment. She always helps me to chose good cheeses, always perfectly well done, to suit the situation in which I want to eat them. She can also advise me on a good wine to accompany the cheese that I want to try.

Jim also has a funny anecdote about an experience in a store. His wife loves spending time in clothing stores when they travel in France. Jim always goes with her and takes this opportunity to practice his French:

> Once, my wife entered a lingerie shop, and spent a very long time choosing and trying on exquisite underwear. During all this time, I was more than happy to chat with one of the saleswomen who was very pleasant and patient, I really had a good

time, but it was the most expensive French lesson that I ever had!

Don't hesitate to go to the local stores, to attend fairs and festivals, and also to use the local services. Many foreigners hesitate to go to the hairdresser, for example, during their stay in France. That is too bad, as chatting with the hairdresser may be an excellent way to learn a few typical French expressions. Again, these people are usually friendly, and they want to please their customers. There is no reason why it should not go well. And they will also probably even pay more attention to make sure that your hairstyle is exactly what you had hoped for because their reputation is at stake. Try to use the local services as much as you can, shop at the open air markets...

This is why it is a good idea, if you really want to immerse yourself into French society for a few days when you travel to France, to stay in a rented apartment rather than in a hotel. The first person you will meet upon arrival will probably be the Airbnb renter (or those from any other rental agency), who will give you information about the neighborhood. It may be your first opportunity to talk with a French person who will most certainly be very patient and helpful.

> *Once, my wife entered a lingerie shop, and spent a very long time choosing and trying on exquisite underwear. During all this time, I was more than happy to chat with one of the saleswomen who was very pleasant and patient, I really had a good time, but it was the most expensive French lesson that I ever had!*
> Jim

In your country, spend time with your French connections

When you are in your own country, in between two trips to France, try to meet as many French-speaking people as you can! Earlier in the book, we gave you the suggestion of meeting regularly with your network of Francophiles or French people. Try to make it a routine, as Jim does. Going regularly to *L'Alliance française* or any other *Centre cultural français*, for example, may be an excellent way to practice your French. These organizations also offer you the opportunity to read various French publications. There may be other places where you can meet French expatriates, especially those who own a small business, such as a *boulangerie* or a restaurant, with whom you may maintain a regular contact afterwards.

If you heed all the above suggestions, if you break the fear barrier, become confident in yourself, and take any opportunity to speak with French people, you will make considerable progress in your overall ability to use the language, which will, of course, make it far easier to overcome other obstacles.

A useful tip to improve your pronunciation

In each issue of our magazine *French Accent*, that you can download on any device, we have several audio links. Each time you click on one of them, you open a webpage on which you can listen to the text related to the audio link: It is usually a glossary or another kind of list of words and/or expressions, a poem, a song, and several French-English scenarios. We advise our readers not only to listen to these audio files, but to practice repeating out loud what they hear, and doing so several times, until they feel confident that their pronunciation is almost as good as what they hear. Of course, ideally, it is better if they can repeat them in front of a French person, or with their teacher, who can correct them. This is an excellent exercise to help you improve your spoken French — and also, almost as important, to help you memorize these words and expressions that you have learned. This is why repeating out loud is a good habit to adopt.

It is the same with anything you listen to in French: audio links in French learning websites, short radio broadcasts, podcasts, short videos on Facebook, etc. If you can try to repeat what you hear, and then listen to it again, you can make progress.

Another step is repeating words or expressions a French person says to you. It may be easier with a friend, but you can also always ask a French person that you find patient and nice if it is OK if you repeat what he/she just said to be sure you will not make a mistake when you say it again. Most French persons will be pleased to help you, unless, of course, you ask them to do so a bit too often, which may annoy them. As we said above, you should appreciate the limits of their patience!...

Finally, do not forget that, as one of our students from Great Britain who is now living in the south of France, John Stonehouse, rightly said in an interview that we published in *French Accent Magazine*: "Communication isn't just about language, it's about attitude, about smiles, about quietly walking away from one's ego, about opening one's heart at least as much as one's mouth, about being interested in people."

> *Communication isn't just about language, it's about attitude, about smiles, about quietly walking away from one's ego, about opening one's heart at least as much as one's mouth, about being interested in people.*
> John Stonehouse, a student of *Learn French at Home*

TO REMEMBER FROM CHAPTER 18

- **You should not miss any opportunity to speak French with French natives**, either in France or anywhere in the world when you have the chance to meet French speaking people.

- **Practice as much as possible with your teacher.** The more you feel confident speaking naturally with him/her, the easier it will be to do the same with other French natives.

- **Listen to the audio links** you may find on the internet, or in the publications of *French Accent Magazine*, **and repeat out loud** every word and sentence.

- **Don't forget that communication is not only language, but also attitude, and smile...**

19. ARTICLES, BOOKS, BLOGS... GET IN THE HABIT OF READING IN FRENCH

AS WE SAID EARLIER, Jim reads in French as often as he can, at least once a day, in the evening, before going to bed. He has done that for several years already, which was a tremendous help in expanding his knowledge of vocabulary and grammar, as well as many aspects of French culture.

> I started with children's books a few years ago, but after some time I could try reading novels. I read slowly because I needed to look up so many words in my dictionary. I find the *Ultralingua* dictionary on my iPhone very effective and useful. My first 'real' book in French was *Le Petit Prince*, by Antoine de Saint-Exupéry, which I have read again and again and that is still one of my favorite books, even if I hate the fact that so many verbs are conjugated in the *passé simple*.

The simple past is a literary past tense, typically used in French literature, that makes life more complicated for most students of French! Jim progressed to reading more and more difficult novels, some of them twice. Among the titles: *L'Etranger*, by Albert Camus, *Hygiène de l'assassin* and *Ni d'Ève ni d'Adam* by Amélie Nothomb,

Monsieur Ibrahim et Les Fleurs du Coran, by *Éric-Emmanuel Schmitt*, etc. The most difficult of all, as it contains a multitude of literary allusions and is full of metaphors, but that he really liked, was *L'Elégance du Hérisson*, by Muriel Barbery. He frequently asked his French teacher for help in understanding a difficult paragraph or passage. The day he turned the last page, he had the feeling of having won a victory!

On some occasions, Jim has made several attempts to read a book, as many as three times for some of them, before understanding them fully. "When I read a book which is particularly difficult, with an advanced vocabulary and grammar, finding the meaning of many phrases or paragraphs is a very slow adventure. It is like a day of sailing — it is very pleasant, but we make very slow progress."

Occasionally, Jim also reads an essay, even though it is not his favorite kind of reading material. For example, he received as a gift an essay, *Le conflit, la femme et la mère* by the French feminist Elisabeth Badinter, which has since been translated into English under the title *The Conflict: How Modern Motherhood Undermines the Status of Women*.

> We were in Paris and it was a surprise present from a very intriguing woman that we met. In reading this book, I learned a lot of things about several issues in France: women and motherhood, gender equality, etc. This was culturally interesting, and a very good exercise to learn French.

Jim also loves reading the weekly satirical French newspaper *Le Canard enchaîné* to which a French friend subscribes. Every Tuesday evening, they have discussions on articles and cartoons, which is an excellent introduction into French culture, and keeps him very well informed about French politics.

When, like Jim, you have reached an intermediate or advanced level, reading a book in French, with the use of a dictionary, is definitely an excellent habit. Read as much as you can, and anything: newspaper articles, books or booklets, or even simply any local advertising. In each case, challenge yourself with some reading and observe the sentence constructions. It doesn't matter if you only understand a small percentage of it.

What is interesting, and useful, is to analyze the word order, the tenses being used, the gender of the words, etc. When you travel in France, going to the local café and reading the newspaper could become a very pleasant daily habit. And when you are in your home country, browse the internet to read French news, subscribe to a newspaper and establish the discipline of reading a full article every other day or every week depending on your time and availability. This is an excellent way of improving your level of French, and your knowledge of French culture.

> *Jim loves reading the weekly satirical French newspaper* Le Canard enchaîné, *which is an excellent introduction into French culture, and keeps him very well informed about French politics.*

Why not try French literature?

A Japanese professor of French and writer, Akira Mizubayashi, who has published several books in French, written in a very refined and beautiful style, explains what reading French literature brings to him:

> ...literature was for me, precisely through the French language, a particular place and space where are brought together, in a luxuriant abundance, projects, hopes, regrets, secrets, expectations, deceptions, joy, sadness, audacity, shyness, avowed or unavowed likings, in short everything that we can probably

gather together under the word *desires* that are linked to life and that link us to life.

We could hardly find a better definition of what reading French literature can bring to a person who is learning the language. It is through literature that you can find the very deepest expressions of those emotions found in every situation in life, and it is also in literature that you can appreciate better how the French people react to these emotions, or to the events that provoked them.

Studying French literature is, therefore, one of the best entryways to French culture. That may also be the case for good French essays, biographies, history books, etc., as long as they are well written and interesting.

As we said earlier, reading a few children's books may be a good start for beginners, as Jim did when he started learning French. Reading a book that has been translated into your language is another idea for a start, as you can refer to the translation each time you have any doubts about the meaning of a certain sentence. Some students do that until they are more fluent: They read one page of a book in French and then read it again in the translation.

An example of an excellent French book that everybody can find in his/her language, as did Jim, is *The Little Prince* (*Le Petit Prince*) which has been translated into no less than 253 languages and dia-

> *It is through literature that you can find the very deepest expressions of those emotions found in every situation in life, and it is also in literature that you can appreciate better how the French people react to these emotions, or to the events that provoked them.*

lects! Most of our students have already read it in their own language, and remember the story, which makes it easier to tackle it in French, and they keep the translation handy to refer to it when/if needed.

You should be aware, however, that if you start reading books that end up being too difficult, even with a good dictionary, it might turn into a discouraging experience. Therefore, to avoid needless frustration, try not to be too ambitious in your choice of what you read. It may be a good idea to ask your teacher for advice on books that you could try to read, according to your level of French. In our online Forum, the students often exchange titles of books that they liked and found accessible.

TO REMEMBER FROM CHAPTER 19

• **Read as much as you can, and anything**: newspaper articles, books or booklets, or even simply any local advertising.

• **Observe the sentence constructions**. It doesn't matter if you just understand a small percentage of it. **What is useful is to analyze the word order, the tenses being used, the gender of the words**, etc...

• **When you travel in France**, going to the local café and **reading the newspaper could become a very pleasant daily habit.**

• **In your home country**, browse the internet to read French news, establish the **discipline of reading a full article** every second day or every week depending on your time and availability.

• **Why not try French literature?** It is in literature that you can **appreciate better how the French people react** in many situations.

• Literature is also one of **the best entryways to French culture.**

20. WRITE IN FRENCH...
AND HAVE SOMEONE CORRECT YOU

"FOR ME, WRITING IS EASIER than speaking," Shinji, one of our most faithful Japanese students, told us.

> I can write easily, at my own pace, even if I always make a few mistakes. But when I speak with French people, I have to listen very closely, understand immediately, and reply right away to continue the conversation. Reading is the most difficult for me, because I cannot understand many sentences even if I look up all the unknown words in the dictionary.

Shinji is an excellent writer and author of very poetic short stories, which is probably one of the reasons why writing is easier for him than speaking. This is also why he has been taking weekly conversation lessons for the past five years. He says that these lessons are a great help for him to be more confident in speaking.

However, he occasionally translates one of his short stories into French, or even writes one in French that he sends to his teacher as homework. The next lesson is, therefore, a discussion during which the teacher explains what changes could be made to the written text. One of the last short stories he wrote was a very funny fantasy, a half reality, a half fiction account of his experiences during a recent trip to Paris.

Jim shares the same feeling. He likes writing, too, and remembers that when he was younger he used to keep a diary. As regards the French language, he says: "For me, writing is easier that talking, because it is not in real time, and the words come more quickly. When I write, I can use my very good friend the dictionary, and look up the words I don't know how to say in French. While, when I have a conversation with someone, I often confuse one word for another."

Homework is vital

Homework is a crucial part of the French learning process and an exercise that will help you improve your writing. As writing is usually not something you can do during a French lesson, either face-to-face with your teacher or through a Skype session, writing exercises are often part of any well-prepared and useful homework.

However, when you speak of homework, the first thoughts that cross the mind of many people are: Homework is difficult, is annoying, takes too much time, is not focused enough on what I need, is useless, etc. This reminds us of a funny quote from the American writer of young fiction, John Green: "I do my [...] homework, and then when I'm done I actually sit with the textbook for like three hours and try to understand what I just did."

Homework is an integral part of any course of study, even for those students who choose to enroll in conversation sessions where there are no specific homework assignment given. They should, at least, read the notes taken during the previous lessons, repeat a few expressions, memorize them and think about using them during another discussion. They may also be asked to read a text or an article in preparation of the next lesson, all of this makes up some kind of homework.

The students should know, first, that assigning homework and correcting it has nothing to do with any sadistic motivation from the part of their teacher to make them suffer, and that it is at least as demanding for the teacher as it is for them. While they are supposed to have an hour and a half homework assignment, their teacher may easily spend the same amount of time, if not more, to prepare it and to correct it. This is because, as it is the case for any lesson, the homework given by the teachers is totally adapted to the students' goals and proficiency level, and also to what they feel comfortable in doing. If the homework is made too difficult, it will discourage the students and will not teach them anything.

This is why, at *Learn French at Home*, the homework is very personalized. Most grammar exercises are created by the teacher on subjects of interest to the student and use vocabulary and idiomatic expressions he/she might particularly want to learn. The teacher uses many of the teaching materials specifically created by the founding team of *Learn French at Home* to help answer the particular needs and questions from the students, such as the magazine *French Accent*, which keeps the readers up-to-date about the latest trends in the French language and culture, and several e-books listed at the beginning of this book. The teachers also use a selection of textbooks, and a wide range of online material to facilitate understanding.

"I think the whole approach is excellent — the on-screen notes, the multimedia content in the homework, and the relaxed style," wrote one of our students, Alan Gow, living in Artfield, UK. Another person, Karen, told us: "I like doing my homework and what I prefer is the *dictées*" (dictations that are published, with an audio link, in every issue of *French Accent* and in a special e-book published by the editorial team: *Write Like a French Person*). "I can listen to them either once or ten times if I have a problem." While Kathy wrote:

> I feel it is very important to do your homework regularly. It not only improves your writing and comprehension abilities but it is also funny how often the things you have just been studying come up in your everyday life. Céline introduces lots of French idioms which help one to speak French colloquially. It really opens up the French language for you.

Jim echoes this idea. He often says that he loves writing essays as homework, and will never miss a chance of writing in French in replying to the *Question du jour* of our online Forum.

All our French teachers can say that they see the difference between a student who regularly does his/her homework, and one who does not. They can see a clear progression in the student. Doing one's homework is also a demonstration of the student's motivation, it stimulates his/her interest, and it is fundamental for absorbing what has been covered in the lesson.

Some students prefer doing their homework right after their lesson to make sure not to forget what they have learned. Others do it just before the next one, as a way of getting ready for the lesson, and some other students work on it a little every day. No matter how they do their homework, it always helps to improve their knowledge and understanding, and is an important reinforcement of what they have learned.

Even for the students who need to work more on listening comprehension than on writing, doing some kind of homework is useful. Karen, from Guernsey, explained:

> My teacher knows where my weaknesses are and structures the lessons to improve on those areas. I am able to complete the homework, which is mostly listening to clips of videos as I need to improve on hearing French spoken and understanding what is being said. There are also exercises to complete relating to the videos, therefore, the more I listen to them, the better it is for me.

Elyette, a young mother who lives in Paris, after having studied with *Learn French at Home*, also said:

> The homework is relevant and appropriate for the lessons I need... I never feel she (her teacher) loses patience with repeat

mistakes and she remembers and really listens. Even her necessary reminders and corrections are subtle and gentle. She is understanding of a mother's needs for flexible hours and, at times, the lack of mental energy for homework, but she still manages to help me make progress. Having the weekly lessons to look forward to, with or without other study time during the week keeps me engaged and learning, and I can tell that I am finally becoming less tongue-tied and more at ease with conversational French, and just as important, more understanding of life in France.

> *I feel it is very important to do your homework regularly. It not only improves your writing and comprehension abilities but it is also funny how often the things you have just been studying come up in your everyday life... It really opens up the French language for you.*
> Kathy, a student of *Learn French at Home*

TO REMEMBER FROM CHAPTER 20

- **Homework is a crucial part of the French learning process** and an exercise that will help you improve your writing.

- If the homework is made too difficult, it will discourage the students and will not teach them anything. This is why, at *Learn French at Home*, **the homework is very personalized.**

21. SOME OF THE HURDLES YOU WILL HAVE TO OVERCOME

THE FRENCH LANGUAGE MAY, at first, appear daunting, as it has many particularities that challenge many people. Here are a few of them, and our suggestions on how to deal with them:

The gender of nouns

"Sometimes I have the feeling that French grammar is the grammar of the absurd," Jim told us.

> ...Especially the gender of words. Who has decided that some of them are feminine and others masculine? Where is the logic? From time to time, my teacher tries to give me some kind of logical explanation, which perfectly satisfies my Cartesian way of thinking.
>
> For example, many words ending in '*e*' are feminine. But there are so many exceptions to this rule that it doesn't help much. Then, she simply says *c'est comme ça* (that's how it is), and that's all I can get.

Indeed, this is one of the major differences between English and French, and it can be quite a challenge that drives many of our students crazy! It is easier for the Germans or Russian students to adjust, or for students who speak another romance language where the nouns also have a gender (even if the gender for the same word often differs from one language to another).

As Jim's teacher said, there are precise rules for many words. For example, among others, the words ending in *ment* (e.g. *gouvernement*), in *al* (*animal*) or in *oir* (*espoir* = hope) are always masculine, and those ending in *ance* (*élégance*), in *sion* (*décision*) or in *ouille* (*grenouille* = frog) and words ending in "*ie*" such as *boulangerie*, are feminine. The majority of nouns ending in "*e*" are feminine but many others are not, such as *groupe* (group) or *parapluie* (umbrella), that are masculine. Sometimes bigger things are masculine and smaller ones feminine, as is the case for *camion* (truck, m.) and *voiture* (car, f.), but *une grue* (a construction crane), which is much bigger than a truck is, nevertheless, feminine... For many words, there is simply no logical explanation. For example, why is *virilité* (masculinity) feminine and *féminisme* (feminism) masculine? Why is *malheur* (misfortune) masculine and *peur* (fear) feminine? Why is *magazine* masculine and *revue*, which has exactly the same meaning, feminine? Idem for *vélo* (m.), and *bicyclette* (f.), which both mean bicycle, or for *profession* (f.), and *métier* (m.), which are two generic terms for a profession.

> *Why is* virilité *(masculinity) feminine and* féminisme *(feminism) masculine?*
> *Why is* malheur *(misfortune) masculine and* peur *(fear) feminine?*
> *Why is* magazine *masculine and* revue, *which has exactly the same meaning, feminine?...*

The only way to avoid making too many mistakes is to try to memorize the most common words. This will take time, but several of our students have told us than after a few months of paying attention to what they read and hear, they see an improvement. "At the beginning, it was terrible. But after a few months it became easier. If we pay attention it comes naturally after a while," one of our American students said. "Now, I find more easily the gender of some words. It is intuitive," another student, who lives in Canada, said.

Anyway, it remains a challenge. We know several people of non-French origin who are totally bilingual, who have even been teaching French for many years and master the grammar often better than some French people, and who still make mistakes with the gender of nouns that a 6 year-old French child would not make. The only thing we can say is: Do not take too much time or trouble with such typical mistakes, and do not worry about it. After some time, and practice, you will know by heart the gender of the most common words.

In any case, the French will always understand what you mean, and not only will they not criticize you or make fun of you, but in most cases they will find it amusing, and cute. This will be part of your charm together with your accent. We would even suggest that you not take too much time trying to figure out the right gender while you are in the middle of a conversation with a French person.

> *Don't worry about making mistakes on the gender of words. This will be part of your charm, together with your accent.*

He/she might be more annoyed if you take too much time trying to find your words than if you use the wrong article to accompany a noun!

The accent marks, and the nasal vowels

This is another specificity, another little difficulty of the French language. At first glance, if may not seem very important. However, if you do not properly use the accents on vowels, not only will you make a mistake while writing in French, but your pronunciation could very well be wrong. The same word can also have a totally different meaning depending on the accent placed on one vowel. For example: *prés* (fields) and *près* (close to), *mais* (but) and *maïs* (corn), *cote* (popularity) and *côte* (coast), or *sur* (above) and *sûr* (certain). It is also very important to be aware of the role of accent marks in verb conjugations. The accent mark will affect the pronunciation of the verb. For example with the verb *espérer* (to hope): *j'espère, nous espérons* (I hope, we hope) or the verb *mener* (to lead): *je mène, nous menons* (I lead, we lead).

The best solution to overcome this difficulty is to learn these accent marks (there are not so many, after all), to memorize them and to learn their function in good pronunciation. Your teacher will help you, and there are many websites for learning French with audio links that you can listen to in order to learn how to pronounce the letters with accent marks.

Equally difficult is to assimilate the pronunciation of the nasal vowels: "*en*," "*in*," "*on*," "*un*," and some other vowel combinations ("*eu*," "*ou*," etc.) — or, worse, groups of vowels and consonants such as "*aille*" or "*ouille.*"

It takes some time to get it, but you should not get too stressed about it and try to make it a fun exercise when you attempt to pronounce some of the more problematic words, such as *moyen* (average), *champignon* (mushroom), *pneu* (tyre), *broussaille* (bushes), or *grenouille* (frog). Doing phonetic exercises with your teacher is often the occasion for a good laugh!

Prepositions: Which ones to use?

The use of prepositions in French, as with other languages, can be very frustrating and it is an ongoing process to learn which preposition to use after particular expressions or verbs. You simply have to memorize them as you go along.

For example, in English we say: "to listen to something," whereas in French there is no preposition used after the verb *écouter*; we also look at something "on television," while in French it is "*à* (at) *la télévision*," etc. Also, in French, the preposition can be different for the same verb depending on its meaning: We say *décider de faire quelque chose* (to decide to do something) and *se décider à* (to make up one's mind).

Pronouns: Which ones to use? Where to put them?

This aspect of the French grammar is probably one of the most difficult, and it usually takes a long time for a student to perfectly assimilate the various pronouns and their placement in a sentence. It is, however, important that you learn the rules for each specific pro-

> *If you do not properly use the accents on vowels, not only will you make a mistake while writing in French, but your pronunciation could very well be wrong. The same word can also have a totally different meaning depending on the accent.*

noun. For example direct and indirect object pronouns are always placed before the verb. We say "I love you" in English, but, as everybody knows, it is *je t'aime* in French.

Therefore, you should never hesitate to ask your French friends for help in case you are not sure which one to use, and where it goes. This is what we did with Jim when he told us, for example, that he particularly liked such or such musician: *J'adore lui*, while he should say: *Je l'adore*... After some time, it became totally natural for him to use the right pronoun, and to put it at the right place, during an improvised conversation.

The conjugation of verbs

Learning how to conjugate the verbs, and especially the numerous irregular ones, is another difficulty of the French language. Most of our students find particularly discouraging the fact that there are several conjugations to use in the past — they particularly have problems with the so-called *passé simple* which is far from being as simple as its name suggests, and is used in French literature, even in children's books. It is also quite difficult for most of them to learn how to use the conditional and, even more, the subjunctive. We fully agree, this is not so easy, and many French people also make mistakes while conjugating verbs.

When we started *Learn French at Home*, we required our students to study this aspect in textbooks, in parallel with getting explanations from their teacher and practicing with him/her as part of their homework. Unfortunately, there are very few language books that explain very clearly how to conjugate the verbs, and the best ones are in French, which is not much help for beginners, and even for intermediate students. The same applies to other problematic aspects of French grammar.

This is why we decided, in every issue of *French Accent Magazine*, to publish an article on a specific grammar point, written in English, and explained as clearly as possible, in non-academic language, with typical examples taken from daily life, scenarios that put the technical explanations in context, and with exercises. In each article, we add audio links so that the readers can listen to the French version of the examples and of the scenarios. As confirmed by several readership surveys that we made, this column is systematically a favorite among our readers. An article which has been among the most appreciated was "How I learned to love the subjunctive."

After several years of writing such articles, we have published a *French Basics* grammar e-book, which is a compilation of most of them and contains more exercises. This e-book, that has become one of the more useful tools for beginners, is in the process of being revised.

A multitude of French idiomatic expressions

This is, perhaps, the most interesting and amusing aspect of the French language, and a very important one, too. The French use so many idiomatic expressions in their daily language, together with many little words that do not always have a very specific meaning, that if you do not know the most common ones you may be completely lost and unable to understand a very simple dialogue between two French people!

> *Very few language books explain clearly how to conjugate the verbs. This is why, in each issue of* French Accent Magazine, *we publish an article on a specific grammar point, written in English, and explained in a non-academic language with typical examples taken from daily life.*

As an example, here is a typical dialogue that might take place between two friends, both students in a vocational school, who are working on an essay their teacher has assigned them:

—Alors Marie, comment ça se passe pour toi, tu t'en sors ?
—Oh, c'est galère[1], je rame[2] un max. Et toi, t'as fini ?
—Bof, j'ai sorti un truc[3] mais ça casse pas des barres[4].
—Il nous en fait voir de toutes les couleurs[5], ce mec.
—Ben oui, il a beau dire que c'est pas la mer à boire[6], c'est quand même pas évident, quoi.
—En tout cas, moi je suis pas sortie de l'auberge[7]. Je commence à en avoir plein les bottes[8].

Literally:
[1] galley
[2] paddle (*ramer* = to paddle)
[3] I took a thing out
[4] it doesn't break bars
[5] he makes us see all the colors
[6] it is not the sea to drink
[7] I haven't left the inn
[8] to have the boots full of it

Translation:
—So, Marie, how's it going for you, you doing OK?
—Oh, it's a pain, I'm having a tough time. What about you, have you finished?
—Nah, I put something down but it's not so great.
—He makes our life impossible, that guy.
—Well, yes, it's useless for him to say that it's no big deal, it's really not at all easy, eh/ya know.
—In any case, as far as I am concerned, I am not close to finishing. I've had it up to here.

Note that in colloquial French, one often leaves off the final vowel in some pronouns and adverbs. In the above scenario, for example, one person says *t'as* fini instead of *tu as* fini. Also, one element of the negative is frequently left off: *ça casse pas des barres* instead of *ça ne casse pas des barres*; *c'est... pas évident* instead of *ce n'est...pas évident*, etc.

Learning new expressions may be fun

Studying the colloquial language used on a daily basis by the French should be part of every French learning program, and it can be truly enjoyable. In every issue of *French Accent*, we publish a few expressions, by theme, in a column called *Le Coin des branchés*. All the teachers also do their best to help their students memorize the expressions they teach them in every lesson, sometimes through an article, a dialogue, a song. Quite often, knowing how to use them in context in a few phrases is part of the homework.

Constantly discovering new and hilarious expressions is a real delight for Jim. He is very attentive to them when he reads French novels and watches French movies, and when his French friends speak together around a dinner table, he listens carefully, and each time he hears an expression that he does not know, he asks them what it means, in what context it should be used, and takes note of it. Later on, he tries to re-use them as often as possible. It has happened several times already that he has surprised some friends by using expressions that very few foreigners know. The last one he learned is *Je m'en fous comme de ma dernière chemise* (I can't care less; lit.: I care no more about it than I do about my last shirt). He also likes *Ça me gonfle* (That gets on my nerves; lit.: That makes me swell up) or *Je me casse* (I'm off, lit.: I'm breaking myself).

Almost all our students tell us, either directly to their teacher or via the online Forum, that they have a few preferred idiomatic expressions. One of our British students, Sarah, told us that the one she likes the most is *Il pleut comme vache qui pisse* (It is raining cats and dogs; lit.: It is raining like a cow that pisses)! One of Mark's preferred expression is *Se mélanger les pinceaux* (To get mixed up; lit.: To mix one's paintbrushes), Sevanh said she found very amusing *Se mettre le doigt dans l'oeil* (To be totally mistaken; lit.: To put one's finger in one's eye) when we published it in our Forum and her favorite expression is *J'ai la pêche* (To be in an excellent form; lit.: To have the peach). Peter said he likes *Chercher la petite bête* (To nitpick; lit.: To look for the small animal), *Avoir le cafard* (To have the blues; lit.: To have the cockroach), and *Faire la grasse matinée* (To sleep in; lit.: To do the fat morning). "It is so expressive," he wrote. "Among other meanings, the word *grasse* means luxuriance and perhaps even decadence."

Nada also found very funny *Avoir un coup de foudre* (To fall in love at first sight; lit.: To receive a bolt of lightening), and most of our students have fun using *Poser un lapin* (To stand someone up, lit.: To put down a rabbit). Raghav particularly liked these three expressions: *Être armé(e) jusqu'aux dents* (To be very well prepared, for example to pass a test, do something difficult, or to get ready for one's French lesson... lit.: To be armed to the teeth), *Avoir mal aux cheveux/ Avoir la gueule de bois* (two ways of saying: To have a hangover; lit.: To feel pain in the hair/to have a wooden mouth), and *Du bout des lèvres* (Reluctantly; lit.: From the tip of one's lips). While Lucy said she liked, among other expressions, *Quand les poules auront des dents* (When pigs might fly; lit.: When chicken will have teeth), and Sylwia

> *There are thousands of idiomatic expressions in French. Studying the colloquial language used on a daily basis by the French can be truly enjoyable.*

finds very funny all the expressions involving animals, especially the more illogical ones, such as *Noyer le poisson* (To confuse the issue, lit.: To drown the fish)!...

We could go on and on with such examples, we can count these expressions by the thousands (a dictionary has compiled some 2,500 of them and the list is certainly not exhaustive), to which can be added a large number of French proverbs. The website "L'internaute.com" has gathered 1,500 of them, but there may be many more (mostly regional proverbs) that have never been listed. We like this one: *Avec du temps et de la patience, les feuilles de mûrier se transforment en robe de soie* (With time and patience mulberry leaves turn into a silk dress, meaning: This is with time and patience that the most beautiful things can be built up), which refers to the traditional industry of silk in the Ardèche region of France, where silkworms were fed with mulberry leaves.

If every language has its own idioms and proverbs, it is well-known that France is among the countries that have a lot of them, and where they are the most frequently used in the daily language. This is why learning the most common expressions is not only very amusing, but useful...

Vulgar or not vulgar?

This is a very difficult question that all our students ask one day or another. When learning French idiomatic expressions, some of them are a bit shocked by the words used, and they don't know if they could really repeat them without insulting the people with whom they speak. They also wonder if these tricky expressions are currently used by everybody, or only by less educated people. This is a sensitive subject for Jim. He recently learned an expression that he found amusing but a little risqué: *Péter plus haut que son cul* (which simply means: To think you're it, you're the cat's whiskers, but literally means: To fart higher than one's ass...). Given the words used, he wondered if this was not too impolite to use it, but he was reassured when he heard a very respectable old lady using it in a very natural way when talking to a few friends. He repeated it in the Forum, but he added that he knows other vulgar expressions that he did not dare to write.

The Japanese professor of French Akira Mizubayashi was also often surprised when he was in France to hear many people speak in a rather gross way, or make extensive use of French slang. For example, a very well educated Frenchman once invited him to his home to listen to a symphony of Gustav Mahler. When he opened his fridge to find a drink to offer to his guest, "he said: *Merde, j'ai que dalle, de la flotte seulement.*" (Shit, I don't have anything, just water).

Many of our students experience the same astonishment when they hear French people talking among themselves and using every few minutes the expressions *Putain !* (Bloody hell, lit.: Whore), *Quel con !* (What a jerk), *Quel bordel !* (What a mess!, lit.: What a brothel!), *J'en ai rien à foutre* (I cannot care less, lit.: I have nothing to f...) or *J'en ai plein le cul* (I am fed up, lit.: My ass is full of it).

Is it vulgar or is it not? Yes, it is a little vulgar, will reply to you a few persons, advising you not to use them yourself with people you don't know very well, as it seems always a little awkward for French people to listen to foreigners using the same informal language, unless they are totally bilingual. At the same time, no, it is not vulgar as it simply belongs to the daily language, and not a single French person, while using them, would think of the meaning of the words — probably because they are widely used. For example, some 30 French idiomatic expressions and 140 proverbs use the word *cul* and most of them are not vulgar.

To help our students, we published a few years ago a list of "Politically correct slang" that they could use, explaining in detail in which context they can do so, and with whom. We also mentioned that many French singers, among those whom the French adore the most, use a lot of slang and rather vulgar idiomatic expressions. As an example, we quoted a few lines of a song by Renaud, *Putain de camion* (Bloody truck), referring to the truck that killed, in 1986, the famous humorist Coluche at the age of forty-two:

Putain de camion (excerpt)

Putain c'est trop con
Ce putain d'camion
Mais qu'est-ce qu'y foutait là
Putain de vie d'merde
T'as roulé dans l'herbe
Et nous, tu nous plantes là...

Translation:
Damn, it's too stupid
That bloody truck
What the hell was it doing there?
What a damned shitty life
You were sent sprawling in the grass
And you leave us behind...

In another issue, in which the main feature theme was "Love in France," we published several lists of common vocabulary, to which we added a list entitled "Be careful with a few tricky words." We took this initiative at the request of several of our students who, once, found themselves in an embarrassing situation by using a common word (such as *baiser*) in a totally improper way, and did not want to repeat the same mistake! One of our students, an Australian middle-aged woman, turned crimson with embarrassment when we told her that, to show her friendship to a nice French guy she met at a party, she asked him: *Je peux te baiser ?* (Can I f... you?). *Baiser* is indeed a very tricky word because as a noun, it means "a kiss*," but it becomes very vulgar as a verb... This is partly why, nowadays, *baiser* is mainly replaced by *bise* or *bisou*. You will notice it when a

---

*The polite way to say "to kiss" is "*embrasser*." You should emphasize the "s" (pronounced like in "mi<u>ss</u>,") if not it may be confused with *embraser* (a "z" sound like in M<u>s</u>) = to "set aflame," which is also ambiguous as it may involve either a fire or a person...

French person with whom you have had a nice discussion says, before leaving: *On se fait la bise ?* (Shall we kiss each other?), and kisses you just on the cheeks. We will come back to this peculiar French habit later in the book.

If, out of ignorance, you curse, or use a swear word that will immediately appear inappropriate, no need to say "Pardon my French!" Not a single French person will understand what you mean... Therefore, it is better not to worry. It is more than likely that the French person who listens to you hides a smile — or tells you kindly in simple words the way to say the same thing a little differently. Remember that one of the things that might really shock a French person (apart from drinking a Coke while you are enjoying a plate full of very special French cheeses) is to interrogate them, before you know them well enough, about their private life!

TO REMEMBER FROM CHAPTER 21

Here are some of our tips to overcome the most common hurdles you will certainly encounter:

- **The gender of nouns: Try to memorize the most common words**. After some time and practice you will make fewer mistakes. And **don't worry too much**, the French will understand you anyway and will simply find it cute!

- **The accent marks and the nasal vowels: Practice a lot with your teacher and with audio links** on websites and on our publications.

- **The prepositions and pronouns: Studying French grammar** will be very useful to know how to use them. If you don't know which ones to use when speaking, **don't hesitate to ask French people for advice.**

- **The conjugation of verbs**: This is another reason why **studying grammar, and having a teacher is essential**. Also very helpful will be **to carefully read our grammar articles** in *French Accent Magazine* and our other publications, in which **all explanations are given in English.**

- **Idiomatic expressions**: The French use a multitude of them, some very funny. This is one of **the most interesting and amusing aspect of the French language! Try to learn a few of them on a regular basis**, pay attention to **the context** in which you can use them, and **to those that might appear inappropriate...**

22. A FEW HINTS TO HELP YOU DEAL WITH THE MAIN DIFFICULTIES WHILE SPEAKING WITH FRENCH PEOPLE

"JANE BIRKIN, THE BRITISH ACTRESS and model who built a career in Paris and married the legendary French singer Serge Gainsbourg, could never remember whether it was '*un baguette*' or '*une baguette*', so she would just order '*deux baguettes*' (two baguettes)." This quote appears in *Bringing up bébé* by Pamela Druckerman, which explains so well the cultural differences between the French way of living and the American and British ones.

Using the plural may be one of the tricks to avoid making a mistake when you are not sure if the word is feminine or masculine. Jim confesses that he does that from time to time, saying that the problem "does not exist in the plural, at least in the spoken language, because the articles are the same." Of course, this cannot work for everything or for very long, but there is no doubt that for people learning French the slightest little trick to avoid a difficulty brings a huge amount of relief. We know that ourselves quite well as all of us (writers and teachers) are at least bilingual, which means that we had to study another language than our native one, and that we had to go through all the same difficulties, anguish, vexations, frustrations — not to mention satisfaction when finally we became more comfortable in our new language!

This is why, during the lessons and through our written materials, we try to help our students to find, from time to time, an easier way to say something. Here are a few more tricks:

Excusez-moi !

If you find yourself having to say something in French anywhere, in a shop, a restaurant or a railroad station, and you are not sure of what you are saying or asking, and you do not remember the appropriate polite form to use (which may happen quite frequently, even if you are an advanced student) don't forget what we said earlier about *excusez-moi* and *s'il vous plaît*... the magic expressions that will help release any possible tension with the person you are talking to.

Prefer *vous* instead of *tu*

We have said this before but it is worth mentioning it again here: You should definitely use "*vous*" instead of "*tu*" when you encounter any adult, unless he/she is a friend, or a child, if you want to avoid finding yourself in an embarrassing situation.

The art of avoiding the subjunctive

The problems you will encounter when speaking with French people are not only linked to the difficulty of finding the right word, or of knowing how to adapt to a particular cultural setting. Conjugating the verbs correctly is another one. We said in the previous chapter that using the subjunctive is a challenge for most beginners and even intermediate students. Even if we repeat to them that it is not so difficult to learn, if they have understood it quite well during the lesson, and if they used it properly in their homework, it happens quite often that, when they are faced with a French person whom they do not know well, they have the feeling that they have suddenly forgotten everything they knew about the subjunctive, and how to use it.

If you find yourself in this position, do not panic. It happens to absolutely all foreigners, therefore the French person you are talking to will not be surprised, and there is always another way to formulate what you want to say: to use the infinitive, or a noun, instead. Note also that you can always shorten your sentence to make it easier, too, as shown in the example below:

You are invited by a French person for dinner but you already have a commitment for the evening (or you do not feel ready yet to spend a full evening speaking French). If you want to decline the invitation, and say something like: "I am sorry, but I can't, I have to go to the train station this evening," you have two possibilities:

—using the subjunctive: *Je suis désolé(e), mais ce n'est pas possible, il faut que j'aille à la gare ce soir.*
—an easier way (using the infinitive and shortening your sentence): *Merci mais désolé(e), je dois aller à la gare ce soir.*

Here is another example: If you want to say: "We will wait until John arrives," you can say either:

—using the subjunctive: *Nous attendrons jusqu'à ce que John arrive.*
—an easier way (using a noun in place of a verb): *Nous attendrons jusqu'à l'arrivée de John.*

Once again, for the French, the most important thing to say is *désolé(e), excusez-moi,* or *merci...*

Asking questions: the easier way

In French, you have several ways of asking questions. In French textbooks and in language schools, you will learn the conventional ones. The most sophisticated and literary way, that the French do not use very frequently in their daily language (you will find it more in literature or in administrative forms), is to invert the subject and the verb. For example: *Parlez-vous anglais ?* (Do you speak English?).

Another possible interrogative form, which is very common, but that some students find more difficult even if the grammar books qualify it as "a simple question," would be to add "*est-ce que*" before the subject + verb + noun/adjective: *Est-ce que vous parlez anglais ?*

This form seems even more complicated for foreigners (though still called "simple" by the textbooks) if they ask a question to someone about somebody else. For example, to ask: Does he speak English?, one has to say: *Est-ce qu'il parle anglais ?*

If you do not have the time to think about the construction of your question, or if you are afraid to make a mistake, there is another, and easier, way. You can simply use normal word order (subject + verb + noun), followed by a question mark and in the spoken language of rising intonation at the end. Most textbooks omit this widely used way of asking questions and ignore the fact that this is the most common interrogatory form. The result is: *Vous parlez anglais ?* And, talking about somebody else, it becomes: *Il parle anglais ?*

Here is another example, with an interrogative adverb: If you are about to take a train at a French station and are not sure of its destination, you want to say: Where is it going? There are three ways to ask this in French:

—*Où va-t-il ?* (adverb + verb + subject).
—*Où est-ce qu'il va ?* (adverb + *est-ce que* + subject + verb).
—*Il va où ?* (subject + verb + adverb). This is the easier way, and you will notice that, in the same situation, this is the one that most French people will use.

There are a few instances where, to make it easier and faster, the French will use a different way of asking the same question. A good example is: If you want to ask what time it is, you should say, in proper French, using the verb *être* (to be): *Quelle heure est-il ?* or *Il est quelle heure ?* But you will notice that most French people will use the verb *avoir* (*to have*) and simply say: *Vous avez l'heure ?* (lit.: Do you have the hour?).

To make it easy, make it short

"Whatever is well conceived is clearly said, and the words to say it flow with ease," wrote the French poet and critic Nicolas Boileau. This quote, well-known by the French people and that they frequently use in the daily language, may very well apply to those learners of French who want to express themselves and are not sure of the right way of doing it. Instead of trying to make long sentences, make them short, replace a difficult phrase by an easier one, go straight to the point. This will be better received by the French person to whom you are trying to say something than in using long and complicated explanations — as long as, if you are asking for something, you do not forget the *s'il vous plaît* at the beginning, or at the end. An example: You are in the Paris Tourist Office, and you want to get a map of Paris. Instead of saying: *J'aimerais avoir un plan de Paris*, or: *Je voudrais un plan de Paris*, you can simply say: *Un plan de Paris, s'il vous plaît*. The person at the counter is supposed to give such maps of Paris to the visitors, so there is nothing exceptional to ask for one.

Another example: If someone asks you where and for how long you have been studying French, try to avoid complicated explanations about the different schools you attended or your travels to France, just summarize, first, by talking about your main experience: *Je suis des cours à l'école depuis deux ans.* = I have been having French lessons at school for two years; or: *J'ai commencé les cours par Skype l'année dernière.* = I started Skype lessons last year. It is only if the person you are talking to asks for more details that you can specify that you did French in high school, and that you went twice on vacation to France, etc.

> *Whatever is well conceived is clearly said, and the words to say it flow with ease.*
> Nicolas Boileau, poet and critic

In summary, the principle is simple: Limit yourself to one short explanation per sentence, and/or to one simple answer to a question. This will encourage the French person to know more about you.

When you are planning your trip to France, we suggest that you prepare a few basic dialogues or scenarios with your French teacher; and when you are not sure how to express your thoughts or share your experience, you should not hesitate to ask your teacher if there is another, simpler way, to say it. This might be the theme of a few lessons, and even of homework. Each time we have done that with our students, we have received positive feedback when they return home. For example, one of our Australian students who loves Carcassonne in south-west France took a few lessons specifically to get accustomed to the easiest and nicest way to communicate with the French about the most important aspects of daily life.

The French, too, make mistakes!

As we already said, you should not think that you are the only one to make mistakes, far from it. Sometimes, when we receive the homework from our students, it happens that we are surprised by the few mistakes they make, compared to what many French people do in letters, emails, or any other postings on social media.

Akira Mizubayashi, who teaches French in a Tokyo University, wrote in 2011: "I must make some very strange mistakes for my francophone friends, but the homework my French students turn in, sometimes makes my hair stand on end."

The phenomenon is not new. Already in the 1980s we remember that a French professor of philosophy, whose students at the university were preparing themselves to become teachers, told us that he could not believe the number of errors he found in their essays. Julien Green, an American writer who was born and died in Paris (1900-1998), who wrote primarily in French, and was the first non-French national to be elected to the *Académie française*, wrote in a book published in 1975: "A letter written in French, without mistakes, surprises today like something of the old times."

There is no doubt that the way French is taught at school in France has evolved over the years in a not so positive way. In the 1960s, the French education system attributed much more importance to a very good knowledge and use of vocabulary and grammar, and the most usual practical exercise was the *dictée* (dictation), very little used today, but which proved much more effective, as almost everybody, even those who had not studied very much beyond primary school, could write a simple text without making any mistakes in the conjugation and agreement of words and had a basic knowledge of the vocabulary.

Nowadays, most of the communication in France is done by email or other quick and easy ways of communications, and very few people take the time to read and correct what they write, which explains — partly — why there are so many mistakes in such exchanges, another reason being that they no longer have this basic knowledge that all French people had in the 1960s. One of the most usual errors is the confusion between the infinitive and the past participle. For example, we often read something like: *On a bien travailler*, instead of *On a bien travaillé* (We have done a good job).

For a foreigner who starts to have a rather good knowledge of French, it is a little reassuring — and it may even be really fun — to see so many mistakes made by French people!

> *A letter written in French, without mistakes, surprises today like something of the old times.*
> Julien Green, writer

In texts, chats, or on Facebook, a quickly composed sort of French

It is even worse with communication by text, chat or Facebook, when everything that goes through the mind has to be sent so rapidly that nobody cares what had been written, provided that the meaning can be understood (which is not always the case, though). This is like if some people write just phonetically, as they pronounce the words, but not as they should be written. Very often, we are stunned by what we read. Obviously, some of the errors that are apparent have been made intentionally, simply to make such communication more fun, as if writing some words in an unusual way was a sort of game. And this is also a way, for the French people, to avoid a few difficulties of their language that they find annoying when they write on their smartphones, particularly the circumflex accent or the cedilla on the letter "c," or the apostrophes, or the double consonants, or mute vowels at the end of words, etc. They also, as much as they can, simply shorten the words.

> *With communication by text, chat or Facebook, everything that goes through the mind has to be sent so rapidly that nobody cares what had been written, provided that the meaning can be understood (which is not always the case, though)...*

Here are a few examples of what we see regularly on Facebook:
—*sa*, instead of *ça* (it);
—*tu menvera*, instead of *tu m'enverras* (you'll send me);
—*y a*, or *ya*, instead of *il y a* (there is);
—*pasque*, instead of *parce que* (because);
—*paré*, instead of *il paraît* (it seems);
—*continu té bien parti*, instead of *continue tu es bien parti* (go on, you're off to a good start);
—*tou com moi* instead of *tout comme moi* (just like me);
—*pi dim tu fé koi ?*, instead of *et puis dimanche tu fais quoi ?* (and then Sunday, what are you going to do?);
—*ta la dal ?*, instead of *tu as la dalle ?* (are you hungry? — in slang);
—*c toi qu'invit ?* instead of *c'est toi qui invites ?* (are you the one who is inviting?).

TO REMEMBER FROM CHAPTER 22

A few hints to help you deal with the main difficulties you will encounter when speaking with French people:

- **Never forget to use** *excusez-moi* **and** *s'il vous plaît* when you have to say something to a French person, anywhere. They are **magic expressions** that will **help release any possible tension** with the person you are talking to.

- **Prefer** *Vous* **instead of** *Tu*.

- **If you want to avoid using the subjunctive, there are other ways.** Read our examples.

- **How to ask questions** might also be a difficulty, as there are several ways to do it. **We have given you the easiest one**, that the French often use themselves.

- Again, **don't forget that French people make mistakes too** — a lot of them. They also have a funny way of communicating by texto or via Facebook...

23. WHEN YOU START NOTICING THE TRUTH ABOUT FRANCE BY YOURSELF

"IF WE CONTINUE LIKE THAT, France will be a new Disney World, it will be France World, people will wear berets and carry baguettes under their arms," Gérard Depardieu said in 2014 in an interview for the French magazine *Le Point*, while he was complaining about the way France is changing (and was justifying his departure from the country for tax purposes). Obviously, such a declaration is very exaggerated, but there is something true about it.

So many clichés are wrong

It is always a surprise for many French people to realize, when reading newspapers or blogs from other countries, the image that some foreigners still have of France. Once, a young Frenchman in his 20s told us that it was by reading an article in an English newspaper that he realized that wearing berets was considered a French custom. For him, it was a Spanish tradition, and he had no memories of seeing a single French person in his family wearing one. You have to browse through very old photo albums to possibly find someone wearing one... When we, as teachers living all over the planet, are invited to a

French fair in Tokyo, Rio, London or New York, we can scarcely believe what we see. As part of a musical act, there are often accordionists who alternate with French cancan dancers — dressed much less sexily than they are in the actual *Moulin Rouge*, one of those French institutions that still exits mainly because of its huge success with the foreign tourists, who make up the majority of its visitors. Croissants are, of course, sold at the food stalls, not always very good, and baguettes, but mainly the soft and squishy type of bread, far from the delicious crusty bread that one finds in France (even if they are far from being good everywhere in France nowadays...).

At the clothing stands they sell a selection of tee-shirts of every color and type with the Eiffel Tower as the main decor, the type not a single French person would dare to wear and then, as unbelievable as it may seem, is the famous beret! Each time we wonder where they came from. There are almost no beret factories in France anymore, except those that supply tourist shops (more and more berets of various colors can be seen in such shops in Paris!), or in the Basque region, where some locals wear them during the folkloric festivals, but there, they are red.

All of this shows that even if most of them are totally outdated, or simply wrong, these old clichés are still very present. Many foreigners are aware of it, especially those who demonstrate a particular interest in France, such as French learners. When we discuss this with our students, most of them find the stereotypes ridiculous, or even insulting. They say that such clichés totally ignore why France appeal to so many people the world over, such as the famous fashion designers, the individual charm of the diverse regions and their different history, as one of our students told us. Other students have also strongly criticized clichés in general, whatever the country they concern, saying that they generate prejudices. We can only fully agree.

Also surprising for French people is to notice how the word "French" is added to things that have nothing to do with France. For example, "French fries" (that are of Belgian origin), "French dressing" (which is far from having anything to do with our usual vinaigrette or any dressing we would make), or "French toast" (even if a few centuries ago French people could eat something similar, called *pain perdu* — lost bread — which was a way of using old bread that was too hard to eat as it was). The first time we heard about "French kiss," it was also a surprise, as no one in France would use such an expression to define what is simply for us a lovers' kiss... Also funny for us is the expression "to take a French leave" (to go AWOL) that the French know as *filer à l'anglaise* (to take an English leave)!

> *It is very surprising for French people to notice how the word "French" is added to things that have nothing to do with France, such as "French fries", "French dressing", "French toast" — and even "French kiss"!*

It is time to make your own judgment

Now that you have reached a sufficient level to understand better what France is about, it is time to get a clear view of the France of your dreams and be realistic about what the country is, and is not.

On the positive side, you will quickly find out that some of the stereotypes that are among the most stupid are totally wrong. If the hygiene in the Middle Ages and during the Renaissance left much to be desired, today French people probably take as many showers as you do. If it is right that French people can eat snails and frog legs, however, in reality very few people serve them nowadays at their tables, unless for very special occasions, and many people do not like them at all. Such meals principally appear on the menus of restaurants that have tourists as their main clientele — we call them *les restaurants à touristes* (restaurants for tourists). Whatever the menu is, we highly encourage foreigners travelling to France to avoid such restaurants as they are far from being the best, as it is the case in many other countries.

On the negative side, another cliché that does not correspond anymore to reality is that the French are far from being as elegant, and thin, as the models appearing in the ads for French perfumes!

There are, however, a few clichés that are totally right. For example, going on strike and demonstrating in the streets are very usual ways to express one's dissatisfaction. Also, most French people have long vacations, take their dogs everywhere (and most of the time do not pay too much attention to the consequences for the sidewalks), and they like wine (they are not the only ones, though). And they also love cheese, but this is something that most foreigners appreciate, too. Jim has a very poetic way to describe his fondness for them: "By eating cheese, one can achieve inner peace, and if we add to it bread and wine, the combination is sublime. If, furthermore, one can eat this work of art while sitting on the *Ponts des arts* in Paris, looking at *L'Île de la Cité*, this is magnificent!"

A similar quote appears in Pamela Druckerman's book, when she said about her husband: One night at a neighborhood restaurant, he swoons when the waiter sets down a cheese plate in front of him. 'This is why I live in Paris,' he declares." OK, this may be a little cliché, but this is also one of the reasons so many people want to learn French.

> *By eating cheese, one can achieve inner peace, and if we add to it bread and wine, the combination is sublime. If, furthermore, one can eat this work of art while sitting on the* Ponts des arts *in Paris, looking at* L'Île de la Cité, *this is magnificent!*
> Jim

We could go on and on scrutinizing each stereotype, and this is certainly what you will do when you travel to France and meet French families, now that you are able to communicate with them. You will, then, discover much more than you could have imagined about France, both positive and negative.

Beyond the cliché: A most interesting perspective

Jill Craig, a University student and contributor to the excellent online magazine *My French Life*™, produced by a community of Francophiles, French natives and expats who seek to move beyond the cliché in analyzing the French lifestyle, wrote, in October 2015, a brilliant article on this very subject. She says that "it's one thing to attempt to experience *la vie française* as a tourist, and quite another when you want to truly immerse yourself. In Paris especially, that's a rather tall order." In this article, she has compiled a list of the key cultural differences they have all encountered and experienced. Below, we reproduce lengthy extracts from this list:

The French... take things a little slower

Although this may not be exactly true when it comes to romantic relationships, we've found that real connections and friendships are a different story — they mature at a much slower rate in France. [...]

One of our very own French correspondents, Jacqueline, nearly made me lose hope entirely when she dryly remarked that 'if you make friends with a French person through your gym, don't expect to be invited to their house after a week... or even a month.' The process will be much slower — but the good news is that when you're (finally) invited, you can be proud!

The French... name-drop much later

Anglophones usually introduce themselves on a first-name basis [...] but this isn't the case in France — first names are not expected.

Generally speaking, the French language has always struck me as much more formal than English — being referred to as *Madame* in a shop still catches me entirely off-guard. But Jacqueline was definite about the importance of this formality: Not being given a first name is not a slight, it's just another cultural difference.

Endearingly, Jacqueline expressed the unease she experienced when the roles were reversed when she lived in the U.S: Being obliged to give her first name felt like a huge intrusion. As she described with a slight shudder: 'I felt mugged — no, really!'

The French expect... *l'apéritif*

This is especially true if you're living somewhere rural, and is an important one to remember: Offer *un apéritif* when a French person calls in. Not to do so is rude, and can be perceived as an insult.

The French are... more private

This equates to basically not asking too many questions (a polite way of saying nosey). This is one of my own personal errors! [...] I ask far too many questions. So, slowly but surely, I am — hopefully — learning to limit them.

It may not seem that you are asking something overly personal, but be sure to define what this means to a French person. Asking how much a car or a piece of clothing costs is deemed rude, not inquisitive.

Indeed, in France, when French people meet for the first time, they do not ask each other anything about their private lives, their work, etc. They would consider it indiscrete, except, of course, if they meet in a professional context as regards information related to their job. We know, this may seem awkward for you, as in most cultures asking such questions is considered to be a polite way of getting to know someone, of showing the person that you care about him/her and that you are interested in what he/she does. For many French people it is taboo, but this is changing somewhat with the new generations who are used to travelling and meeting foreigners, and are much more open-minded.

The opposite can be true for you: Just because French people seem to be disinterested in you and your personal life does not necessarily mean that they are not interested in you as a person. They are just being discrete.

> *When French people meet for the first time, they do not ask each other anything about their private lives, their work, etc. They would consider it indiscrete.*

Therefore, if you are not well acquainted with the French people you encounter, you should avoid asking such questions spontaneously. It is only when the French begin to talk about such or such an aspect of their life, or if they are the first to ask you a personal question, that it will be OK for you to do the same.

Even so, many French people will always have a tendency to prefer speaking between themselves, even if they know each other quite well, of anything other than private matters (and even less so about their feelings), such as something they read in the news, any event linked to their job, their hobby or any cultural or sports interests they may have, etc.

Jill Craig continues on other aspects of the French character:

The French are… fond of giving less information rather than more

Les Français seem to find lots of questions and enthusiastic greetings *trop américains,* and very off-putting — even false. It bewilders them when an Anglophone feigns interest in every aspect of their life, such as their job, family, their day [...].

The French are… not over-sharers

Our next tip is to avoid over-sharing at all costs. People worldwide find it uncomfortable, but with all the formality, the French are even more aware of social barriers. *De temps en temps,* it still feels like I'm pulling teeth with my boyfriend over dinner. He doesn't see the need to 'discuss every detail of his day' — and I want to hear all about it.

The French are... aware of current affairs

In my experience, the French are much fonder of discussing current affairs than other people [...]. Cultural and social issues are important in France, as are your opinions on these and it comes up often in French conversation — so keep up to date!

It doesn't take much out of your day, so check out *Le Figaro*, *Le Monde*, or even *BBC France* and form your own opinions. And be prepared to defend them!

The French... do not consume in excess

Not that we're in any way suggesting that you are — but personally, I've sometimes been a little nervous at a party and sipped too enthusiastically on a glass of wine. It's a mistake, because it means I have less control over my French, which doesn't help the situation in any way...

So at a party, don't drink too much. It's frowned upon, and will single you out as being not French. I was once told that it was very *'provincial'* to drink heavily — oh, the shame!

The French... don't take kindly to criticism

This one isn't really a cultural difference so to speak, because hardly anyone likes to hear their country and people insulted — but it's important nonetheless. Don't think you can bond with people by insulting things you have personally found annoying throughout your day, like the local customs, or shops being closed at certain hours. It can be seen as a slight against French ways.

So, *en bref*, don't be rude, and avoid criticisms: saying 'back home, we do it this way' is simply annoying. [...]

French ways may often differ to those of their Anglophone counterparts, but they shouldn't be automatically dismissed as cold, or unfriendly in any way. It's quite simply a matter of different rules of courtesy, and respecting them will definitely pay off.

> *French ways may often differ to those of their Anglophone counterparts, but they shouldn't be automatically dismissed as cold, or unfriendly in any way. It's quite simply a matter of different rules of courtesy.*
> Jill Craig, contributor to *My French Life*™

To see France, and the French, from another perspective

"You never really understand a person until you consider things from his point of view... Until you climb inside of his skin and walk around in it." This quote from Harper Lee in *To Kill a Mockingbird* is very appropriate to getting acquainted with people from another culture, too.

It is always interesting to hear our students' first impressions when they come back from France. When one of our Japanese students, Tomomi, who had never been to France before but who had acquired quite a decent knowledge of basic French, travelled to Paris on a business trip, her teacher was a little worried because she had such huge expectations. Before her trip, her teacher devoted entire lessons, not only to have her repeat the usual expressions she might have to use with French people, but to try as much as she could to prepare her for any possible cultural shock. She described everything negative or shocking that she might witness or encounter. When Tomomi came back and had her first lesson after the trip, she exclaimed with joy: "It was so wonderful! I love Paris! I love the French! Everything went so well, everybody was so nice with me, I couldn't believe it. It was the best experience I have ever had in my whole life. Now I can't wait to go back and stay longer..." This is a demonstration that the fact that you speak a little French, added with a minimum of preparation, can make a major difference!

Most of our students who have returned to France a second or third time after having considerably improved their French tell us that, now, they see the country and the French from another perspective. However, the reactions are not always so positive.

Even Jim acknowledged this fact in April 2005:

> The danger, when we better understand the French language and culture, is that we see more clearly the negative aspects of the country, or of the French people. Now I am more aware of

the rather negative changes in the country. For example, it becomes sometimes difficult to find a good restaurant, I know that we definitely have to avoid the touristic parts of Paris, and do more research than a few years ago to find a good restaurant. Sometimes, when I understand something that sounds negative, I feel like saying: 'No, not that! This is not the France of my dreams.'

However, he added: "Don't forget the kindness of the French people. Yes, I mean it. Contrary to what some other people say, I find them nice. It is not a 'smiley-face' culture like in the US, but, most of the time I find that the people are quite warm."

> *I love Paris! I love the French! Everything went so well, everybody was so nice with me, I couldn't believe it. It was the best experience I have ever had in my whole life.*
> Tomomi, a student of *Learn French at Home*

Could the French malaise be "a bitter wisdom?"

Another possible disappointment comes from the confirmation of the pessimism of many French people, which may come as a shock to foreigners who still have the image of France as being the country of the *joie de vivre*. Even if this aspect of this way of thinking is sometimes included among the known clichés, it can come as a surprise. Of course, it does not happen all the time, and the French can also be very enthusiastic, but you will certainly notice, when speaking with them, that they are quick to criticize (a film, an article, the action of government officials, a reform, etc.) and that they can be very negative with regards to the future. It is true that there are not very often happy endings in French literature or movies. In many cases, French books and films do not end with "and they all lived happily ever after." It is even the case for children's books, remarked Pamela Druckerman. "The French book is more like real life," she wrote.

Obviously, the tendency of the French to be quite realistic does not encourage them to see the world through rose-colored glasses! Some students find it difficult to deal with it, some others try to demonstrate that their negativism is not always justified (especially when the French criticize their world-acclaimed social security system and the free education). But they will quickly realize that it is mainly a facade and that the French will be the first to react against any serious criticism on their country coming from outside, and that this is more the expression of a mood than of a deep dissatisfaction or unhappiness.

According to the economist Claudia Senik in her book *L'économie du bonheur*, quoted by Florence Harang in the online magazine *My French Life*[TM]:

> French unhappiness isn't linked with objective circumstances, but rather with the values, beliefs and perception of reality that the French have... It is the result of a cultural phenomenon relating to representations or manners of being that have been handed down from generation to generation, even if their causes have disappeared.

The well-known British journalist Roger Cohen has another interesting approach to the supposed French pessimism. In an Op-ed published in 2013 in *The New York Times*, *France's Glorious* Malaise, he noted:

> I have been reading a lot about the existential anguish of France [...] If moroseness is a perennial state, rather than a reaction to particular circumstance, does it really matter? The

French are living off their malaise much as the British live off the royal family. It's a marketing ploy with its degree of affectation; an object of fascination to foreigners rather than a worrying condition.

He went further by giving a few interesting examples:

Tell a Frenchman what a glorious day it is and he will respond that it won't last. Tell him how good the heat feels and he will say it portends a storm. I recently asked in a French hotel how long it would take for a coffee to reach my room. The brusque retort: 'The time it takes to make it.' This surliness is more a fierce form of realism than a sign of malaise. It is a bitter wisdom. It is a nod to Hobbes's view that the life of man is, on the whole, 'solitary, poor, nasty, brutish and short.' Nothing surprises, nothing shocks (especially in the realm of marriage and sex), and nothing, really, disappoints. Far from morose, the French attitude has a bracing frankness. No nation has a more emphatic shrug. No nation is the object of so

> *Nothing surprises, nothing shocks (especially in the realm of marriage and sex), and nothing, really, disappoints. Far from morose, the French attitude has a bracing frankness.*
> Roger Cohen, journalist

much romanticism yet so unromantic itself. No nation internalizes as completely the notion that in the end we are all dead. Now, it is true that France lives with high unemployment in a depressed euro zone;... that it is chronically divided between a world-class private sector and a vast state sector of grumpy functionaries; that its universalist illusions have faded as its power diminishes... Still, moroseness is a foible in a country with superb medicine, good education, immense beauty, the only wine worth drinking, an army that does the business in Mali, strong families and the earthy wisdom of *la France profonde*.

French people have a complex personality

Years of teaching foreign languages has brought home to us that the complexity, or the specificities, of populations, are reflected in their language. This is certainly the case for the French. "The more precise image of the French spirit is the French language itself," the French writer and politician Désiré Nisard wrote.

The French language is quite complex, full of paradoxes and the exceptions to the rules are often confusing. The attitude of French people can be confusing, too, for foreigners. Contrary to some other cultures where either the religion, the traditions, or feelings and pride of belonging to a community or a country are strong enough to be reflected in a sort of generalized foreseeable attitudes that their population has, the French are very much unpredictable in their behavior and reactions to anything. And they are full of paradoxes. We have devoted numerous articles of our publication *French Accent Magazine* to this important subject.

For example, in an article published in August 2013, entitled "The French don't do anything (well, hardly) like other people!", we explained that, among other paradoxes:

...the most surprising fact is the rebellious spirit that all of the French are imbued with in a country that is so highly controlled by rules. There are thousands of laws, judicial codes (civil, administrative, penal, etc. — there are more than 60 different sets of codes!), decrees and administrative orders. In addition, all those who exercise some kind of power in society (company executives, directors of associations, salespeople, teachers, members of the medical profession) invent and impose their own rules, and governmental authorities have conjured laws and rules that apply to practically every activity in life and of society (the dates of the semi-annual sales, the opening times for stores, Sunday closings, the minimum wage for each profession and craft, the statute of each small association, etc.). However, to attempt to bypass these rules, laws and regulations or to prevent the execution of a law is a national sport.

If they at times appear cold in their social interactions, the French are always ready to sympathize with and to exhibit a complete sense of solidarity when they meet someone who is

> *For the French, to attempt to bypass laws and regulations or to prevent the execution of a law is a national sport.*

having a conflict with the authorities, and they are ready to lend a helping hand. They can also exhibit a really strong sense of solidarity among themselves in times of crisis. This was the case after the terrorist attacks in Paris, first of all against the satirical magazine, *Charlie Hebdo*, which united almost the entire country, and then again following the attacks of November 13, 2015.

> *The French can exhibit a really strong sense of solidarity among themselves in times of crisis. This was the case after the terrorist attacks in Paris.*

There exists, however, a surprising paradox, just one of the many, in the fact that most French people become almost totally docile and obedient when, for example, it is a matter of listening to the advice of their doctor. And, it is also said that the French have a dependent relationship to government agencies. That is to say that many people expect governmental agencies such as Social Security, employment services or their labor unions, among others, to find solutions to their problems rather than working things out by themselves.

These are a few examples of the charming complexity of the French. Therefore, it is not surprising that a foreigner visiting France can be frustrated or a little perplexed by some of the attitudes expressed by the French. One could even say that when you encounter a French storekeeper or a waiter, for example, you never know how they will react to a request or a question!

In any case, travelling to France when you speak better French may encourage you to be more interested in many other aspects of French culture. In following Jim's example, it may be fascinating for you to expand your knowledge by listening to intellectual, historical or political blogs, reading *Le Canard enchaîné*, and having real conversations with French people about any aspect of France that you would like to understand better and, by doing so, eliminating once and for all the stereotypes and wrong impressions that you may have had before you could speak French fluently.

TO REMEMBER FROM CHAPTER 23

- **Many clichés about the French are totally wrong.** Some are not. It is time to make your own judgment.

- **Now you can see France, and the French, from another perspective.**

- **The French** take things a little slower, they **are more private**, and fond of giving less information rather than more.

- **They are very much aware of current affairs.** Cultural and social issues are important in France.

- **And if the French malaise was in reality "a bitter wisdom?"**

- **The French**, along with their language, **have a very complex personality**. They are very much unpredictable in their behavior and reactions to anything, and they are full of paradoxes.

24. HOW TO DEAL WITH THE DIFFERENT PHASES OF DISCOURAGEMENT

AT A CERTAIN STAGE OF YOUR STUDY of the language, you may very well have the feeling that you are not making any more progress, and feel discouraged. Discouragement is a natural feeling that can happen to anybody, whatever your goal, whatever the efforts you have made so far. The Canadian writer, university student and entrepreneur Scott H. Young, who, among other projects, met the challenge of learning four languages while travelling to several countries without using any English, wrote in his blog: "One of the most important meta-skills for becoming good at anything is being able to push through the frustration barrier." A feeling that may occur when "you haven't reached the level of proficiency where you can actually enjoy it. A perfect example is learning a foreign language," he added.

> When I started learning French, the process was difficult. Speaking French wasn't enjoyable. I had difficulty understanding simple things and the effort wasn't rewarding. Now, I'm still not fluent, but I actually enjoy French. I'm reading my first novel in the language (*The Count of Monte Cristo*) and I'm currently spending my winter holidays with a Belgian family,

speaking French exclusively. These are experiences I wouldn't have enjoyed if I had got stuck at square one.

Suddenly, after a few months or years of studying French, you may very well have the feeling that you have reached a plateau and that you are stuck there. This happens to so many students that it is important to prepare yourself for it. We could simply say: Do not accept to remain stuck, move forward, there is no doubt that you can do better!

However, we also know that it may be easier said than done. Below are a few suggestions on how to get through this difficult stage.

Stop, and take the time to reflect

The first thing to do, when you are faced with any strong feeling of frustration or discouragement, is to acknowledge it, to accept it, and to reflect on it. Why do you have this feeling? Is it true that you are stuck at a plateau?

If you take the time to observe the progress you have made since the beginning, you may, on the contrary, realize that you have learned a lot already, that you feel much more confident speaking or writing, that you understand better what French people tell you. Then, you could look back at your initial list of goals and take the time to observe in depth what you have achieved already, where you are on the ladder of success. This will certainly make you realize that you have progressed considerably along the path towards the goals that you had set for yourself. The simple fact of reviewing your personal objectives might be enough to give you the motivation to go further. Would it not be too bad to have reached this stage and not continue?

We know very well from experience than such a phase of discouragement is just a temporary one. It is simply part of the ups and downs that are a part of any undertaking in life. "It's not as if our lives are simply divided into light and dark," the Japanese novelist Haruki Murakami says. "There's a shadowy middle ground. Recognizing and understanding the shadows is what a healthy intelligence does." This is a phase you will probably all go through, and there is no doubt that, even if you are not totally aware of it, you are indeed moving forward towards your goals.

Jim told us that learning French "is definitely not a straight line. It seems that I spend long periods without making any progress and then, suddenly, my level has improved." His experience is a demonstration, among many others, that there is no such thing as reaching a point where you no longer move ahead. Many grammar rules, vocabulary or expressions that you have not fully absorbed along the way will come back to you naturally, when it is time, when you are ready to assimilate them. Do not let this feeling of discouragement take over your initial enthusiasm. And remember, as we have said before, that the fact that learning French is not that easy will give you one more reason to be very proud of your achievements...

> *It's not as if our lives are simply divided into light and dark. There's a shadowy middle ground. Recognizing and understanding the shadows is what a healthy intelligence does.*
> Haruki Murakami, novelist

Remember the joy you have encountered at each step of your progress

First, something to remember: the joy of any little accomplishment you have made so far. Our student Marion Stonehouse explained it in a lyrical way during an interview she gave to the editors of *French Accent Magazine*:

> Language is the key to integration. How could it be anything else? I had very little French and was very inhibited. We found it was like learning to swim; if you stand on the edge of the pool and dip in your toe you never get to swim. If you jump in and flounder about it's uncomfortable but you survive. When you are really in trouble somebody comes to the rescue. It's only by constantly trying that you improve. Having said that, it is tiring, but it's also very rewarding and above all it's fun. There is the excitement of listening to someone talking in the café and you suddenly realize you understand what they are talking about. We rush home to tell each other that we have used a phrase or expression we used in our lesson and it worked! I think Michel Thomas summed it all up when he said 'You have to be brave.'

Acknowledge what you have already assimilated

This is, in fact, though the teaching by the polyglot and linguist Michel Thomas (1914-2005) that we can draw the first lesson on how not to let oneself be affected by discouragement: "What you understand, you know; and what you know, you don't forget."

Even if you continue to make mistakes, you have progressed, it is important to acknowledge it. "My spoken French has progressed greatly within the last year as well as my understanding," Shelley Ruddock said. Then she added:

> When speaking to new people, I still feel very conscious of making mistakes and perhaps giving people the wrong impression of myself. This doesn't ever stop me from speaking to people, but at times I think 'Oh no, did I say that in the right way?!' or 'Oh no, they are looking at me rather oddly now!'

However, she is proud of the progress she has made:

> I used to avoid bumping into our local farmer because I was embarrassed about making a fool of myself; he speaks with a strong local accent, very hard to understand at times. But now when I see him we stop and chat for a while, exchange news and weather reports! And often come away having learnt a new word or two!

Don't be stuck by limits you have imposed on yourself

"Challenge, conflict, confusion and uncertainty are beautifully orchestrated vehicles for our growth," Robin Sharma says. "As you meet your limits, your limits will expand," he adds. "The only limits on your life are those you set yourself," he also reminds. "Relentless learning is one of the main traits of an open and powerful person."

Another author and motivating speaker, Dr. Steve Maraboli, confirms the temporary character of the limits you may think you have reached: "Our limits are not permanent barriers or walls; they are reference points, markers that are meant to be moved or exceeded according to our goals." The same ideas are expressed by the writer Zhena Muzyka: "Limits are like guardrails carefully lining the road leading to your dream." She added: "Paradoxically, working with limitations makes your dream more accessible."

> *Challenge, conflict, confusion and uncertainty are beautifully orchestrated vehicles for our growth... As you meet your limits, your limits will expand.*
> Robin Sharma

Don't forget that mistakes and obstacles are part of the experience of learning a language

Steve Maraboli also says: "Those who are successful give credit to their mistakes and give them a polished new name, experience." Several of our students admit that the difficulties they are faced with at each stage of learning are fully part of the experience of learning a new language. Many of them approach this philosophically, like James and Elma Durrand, who told us that they "had learned that with patience most minor obstacles take care of themselves."

Take a break

It goes for language learning as for any undertaking in life. When you have the feeling that you are overwhelmed, or that you are totally stuck and feel that you are not making any progress, why not close your French textbook, tell your teacher that you are taking one or two weeks break, and just think about something else for a little while? There is no need at all to approach a state of burn-out by being too obstinate or insisting on going too fast when you obviously cannot devote enough time to your study and when you feel discouraged because you realize that you will not be fluent as soon as you were anticipating. Provided that this break not last too long, it might regenerate you, give you the impetus you were missing, and it may also very well help you to realize the progress you have already made. You will then be able to go back to work with a relaxed and more positive attitude. As the Singaporean life coach Malti Bhojwani said in her book *The Mind Spa: Ignite Your Inner Life Coach*, "Relaxing after intense effort not only provides an opportunity to rejuvenate, but also to metabolize and embed learning."

Also, taking a break and giving yourself all the time you need to relax and pamper yourself is typical of the French way of thinking! As you know, resting, napping, taking long weekends and vacations are priorities for all French people, therefore your French teacher will certainly understand you when you make this request to him/her, when you feel the need for it!

Revise, again and again

"Sometimes you have to take a step back to move forward," wrote the American author Erika Taylor in *Moving Forward*. One of the best ways to improve and not get stuck at a basic level without evolving is to go back to what you have already learned, and to revise. Forgetting is part of the process of learning, it is a totally natural phenomenon that happens to all students.

This is why revising, reviewing regularly what you have learned but that you may have forgotten, is essential. Jim likes to joke about it, saying that it is only after he has made the same mistake a hundred times that he can get it right. Of course, this is just a joke, he

> *There is no need at all to approach a state of burn-out by being too obstinate or willing to go too fast when you obviously cannot devote enough time to your study and when you feel discouraged because you realize that you will not be fluent as soon as you were anticipating.*

learns much faster than that, but it confirms, from his experience, that it is only through revision and repetition, that you can assimilate what you are learning.

This is why, when you are in a phase of discouragement, going back to what you have learned and forgotten will help you memorize better, and improve. This will also demonstrate to you that you have progressed more than you thought, and may very well give you the courage to move on.

Don't give up and move on!

Now that you have realized the progress you have made since you started, that you understand that there is no such point where you remain stuck, that learning can only be progressive, that you constantly evolve even if you are not always aware of it, and that you have taken the time to take some rest and to recharge your batteries, you will certainly have regained the energy and willpower that you had at the beginning. Then move on! Listen to the encouragement given by the Alaskan-born writer and blogger Seth Adam Smith: "If you're feeling discouraged and defeated — don't quit. Play on, hope on, and move forward. The music you play — even in the midst of incredible darkness — can and will turn the tide of your own battles."

You could also revive your dreams and motivations, and follow the example of the writer and motivator Edmond Mbiaka: "I have some strong positive reasons why I am on the path that I am, and this is why moving forward is the only option that my mind sees."

> *I have some strong positive reasons why I am on the path that I am, and this is why moving forward is the only option that my mind sees.*
> Edmond Mbiaka, writer and motivator

TO REMEMBER FROM CHAPTER 24

You may very well feel a little discouraged at a certain point in your learning. Here are our suggestions on how to overcome this very natural feeling:

- Stop, and take the time to reflect.

- Remember the joy you have encountered at each step of your progress.

- Acknowledge what you have already assimilated — much more than you think.

- Don't be stuck by limits you believe you have reached. This is a wrong impression.

- Don't forget that mistakes and obstacles are inevitably part of the experience of learning a language.

- Take a (short) break.

- Revise, again and again.

- Don't give up and move on, now that you have recharged your batteries!

25. GET READY FOR YOUR TRIP OR MOVE TO FRANCE

WHEN ASKED WHAT ADVICE Jim would give to someone who is learning French but has not been to France yet, he replies:

> Learn how to say the following things in French: Please; thank you; hello; goodbye; where are the toilets (plural, not singular)? I would like (not I want); the name of a French wine you like (not just red or white wine); coffee; the check please; I'm sorry; excuse me. Bring a phrase book and a small translation dictionary. Never begin a conversation in English, even if your French is terrible. Never begin a conversation with the words 'Do you speak English?' Say hello to the shopkeeper when you enter a shop and goodbye when you leave.
>
> Above all these things, realize that you are a guest in someone else's country, and that it is up to you to adapt to their culture, not the reverse. If you follow the above advice, you will hopefully have a great time and find France and the French people charming.

As we said earlier, learning French (or any other language) is learning the culture of the country and being willing to respect, and at least partly follow, the often unwritten rules of behavior or etiquette like those that Jim summarized.

If you do so, then you may just forget about your fears and apprehensions and just go with the flow, open your eyes, ears and heart to discover France as if you had always lived there. Simply strolling around the streets of Paris can be a wonderful experience. This has always been Jim's experience during each of his trips.

> The city itself is beautiful, the food is great, there is a *fromagerie* on every corner, and a bottle of good Bordeaux is still cheap. We have been to Paris many times, and we always find something new. Did I forget to mention the baguettes, croissants, *bistros*, bars, parks, museums, aperitif-time, dining at a sidewalk café? The list goes on and on.

Asked what a perfect day in Paris is for him, he replies:

> One of my favorite things to do in Paris is nothing. By nothing, I mean just wandering around with only a vague plan of where to go and stumble upon something great. I especially like the French word *déjeuner*. It's not just a noun, but also a verb — I think that this says a lot. In English, we don't have this verb, we need other verbs just to help us have lunch... We need to have lunch in Paris to truly understand its significance. Breakfast (espresso and croissants in our favorite café in Auteuil), walking around the city, lunch in another café or a picnic in a park, more walking, maybe a museum hit, *apéro*-time, dinner in a great *bistro*, walking after dinner, metro home — this is a good day.

Always start with *Bonjour!*

As soon as you feel ready to take that leap of faith and stay for a longer period of time in France, then it is time to take the initiative to speak with the locals, whether in Paris or anywhere else in the country. As we explained in a previous chapter, this is one of the best ways to improve your French. This is also an excellent way to immerse yourself even more into the French culture and observe it with a more objective eye.

The most important will be to start, in all cases, with *Bonjour*. We already mentioned several times the importance of the few expressions that are always part of everyday dialogues when meeting French people. A very interesting explanation of the importance of *bonjour* in France is given by Pamela Druckerman:

> I think tourists are often treated gruffly in Parisian cafés and shops partly because they don't begin interactions with *bonjour*, even if they switch to English afterwards. It's crucial to say *bonjour* upon climbing into a taxi, when a waitress first approaches your table in a restaurant, or before asking a salesperson if the pants come in your size. It signals that you view her as a person, not just as someone who's supposed to serve you. I'm amazed that people seem visibly put at ease after I say a nice solid *bonjour*. It signals that — although I have a strange accent — we're going to have a civilized encounter.

> *I'm amazed that people seem visibly put at ease after I say a nice solid bonjour. It signals that — although I have a strange accent — we're going to have a civilized encounter.*
> Pamela Druckerman, journalist and writer

Even adding a *Monsieur* or *Madame* onto *bonjour* will demonstrate your respect towards that person.

On the contrary, if you forget to say *bonjour* (which happens to the French, too, from time to time) the salesperson you hope will help you may very well pretend that he/she has not noticed that you were there, or may drag his/her feet, or prove not to be really helpful. It sometimes happens that he/she, before letting you finishing your question, interrupts you with a blaring *Bonjour !* to make sure you got the message. In such a case, you have no other choice than to say the magic word in turn, and start again what you were trying to say.

Do not forget to say *au revoir* (good bye), either. In a café or restaurant, even if you have already paid your bill, it would be considered very rude not to say good bye to your waiter/waitress or, if he/she is not there or is in the back of the room, to say it to whatever bartender or other member of the staff is there. You will get an *Au revoir, merci !* in return.

Try to speak French like the French

Another important thing is to remember, and practice, that you have certainly already learned with your teacher, and/or with your French friends: to use, as much as possible, a simple and common language and avoid academic French. Akira Mizubayashi wrote that once, the director of a language training center in France told him that he was surprised by the accuracy of his French, mentioning that he "spoke like a book," adding that "this was a compliment, not a reproach. Was it really a compliment? I am not so sure. What is certain, in any case, is that my oral French lacked a natural quality... It was entirely shaped by my learning how to write French."

Choosing the right words, the right way of expressing yourself while speaking with French persons, is definitely a challenge because it is not always easy, when you are not yet totally familiar with the language, to be certain about how to strike the right balance between academic French and a too familiar language. Several students have expressed this fear of becoming too familiar and of using expressions that would seem awkward and out of place for a foreigner.

The only way to know how to find the proper mix is to take the plunge: to listen to conversations between French people, and see how the people react when you speak, and not to hesitate to ask them if what you have said is correct when you notice a surprise on their part. In any case, it should not be a major problem. Only experience will teach you the best way to express yourself — and, as we have already said several times, if you make a little faux pas you simply risk triggering a smile of amusement. This may even break the ice (while talking with people who are as shy as you) because you should know that the French may be as timid as you during the first encounter.

Be prepared for frank remarks and some rudeness

The shyness of French people is sometimes one of the causes of this well-known reputation of rudeness that some of them demonstrate at first. Our Japanese student Shinji has, on several occasions, been shocked by the coldness of some waiters, particularly in restaurants for tourists, and of a few shopkeepers. However, he understood quickly that the rather cold attitude at the beginning was often caused by some kind of shyness on the part of a shopkeeper who was not sure what he was asking, or surprised by the question, or who felt embarrassed about not being able to satisfy his request. After a while, when the misunderstanding was solved, the shopkeeper was visibly more relaxed and pleasant.

It should be pointed out, though, that something specific to the French is the frankness with which some of them speak to you, that you see less in the English-speaking world, or in Asia. This will be not so obvious with your French friends, who will certainly do their best not to hurt you with unpleasant comments, but you can expect to encounter some attitudes from shop owners or restaurant waiters wherever you go. Not everybody is the same, or has the same experience, but you have to be ready for it, and not make a big deal about it. Our British student Seona Reilly who settled closed to Paris, while explaining how she likes her life in France, mentioned in an interview: "Overall, I find the French friendly and helpful (unless they work in retail or the service industries!)," and she added: "Customer support can be inflexible and unreliable."

Indeed, you might, from time to time, be offended by some unpleasant demeanor or reactions, but, as Jim says, such attitudes can also be witnessed in other countries:

> On the surface, the French are more reserved than the Americans. But, fundamentally, I find that the French are very warm and generous. Sometimes they have the reputation of being cold, or even snobbish, but from my experience I have found the contrary. From time to time I can meet someone who is grumpy, but no more than in the US. Most of the time I find the French charming and great. I think that this reputation is based on a cultural misunderstanding more than on a real character trait.

France: the best country in the world for foreign students

In January 2014, Paris was identified as the "Best city in the world for students" by QS, a specialized British Company. According to another poll made for Campus France by TNS-Sofres, the main French research institute, France is the country as a whole that is praised by foreign students: "Ninety one per cent of the students who participated in the poll declared they were satisfied or very satisfied with their stay in France." In an article published on January 4th, 2014, in *M Le Monde*, many interviews of students were cited. Here are a few excerpts:

—"A marvelous and magnificent country. You have to have lived elsewhere in order to notice it," Yana Tarasovo, a Russian student, said.

—"Nature has been generous with France... You have the best transport system in the world!," commented Parth Joshi, from India.

—"In France, there is a vision of life which is quite balanced. One sets aside time for one's private life and leisure. Success is not only based on one's career. The family, friends, are also very important. I find that rather positive," a Chinese student, Lin Xiang, said.

—"Compared to my country, politics is very much a part of many discussions. When we go to a party in France, people talk about it in a natural way. In Brazil, this bores everybody, you will be told: 'Politics, it is always the same thing.' Here, there is a great political conscience," explained Roberta Lima, from Brazil.

—"Philosophy is totally integrated into the society. One can find all the books of the major philosophers in bookstores. In the United States, you would have to order them online. And philosophy is taught already in high school in France! It may be the only country to do that and I find that terrific," Donald, an American student in Paris, added.

> *In France, there is a vision of life which is quite balanced. One sets aside time for one's private life and leisure. Success is not only based on one's career. The family, friends, are also very important. I find that rather positive.*
> Lin Xiang, Chinese student

Those who have chosen to settle in France

> We admire the social graciousness of the French, the *'bon appétit'* from fellow diners, the daily greetings and *bises* on our way through the village, the friendliness of the local children who receive affection from family and friends with quiet dignity and confidence, and the importance attached to the family which is so essentially French. It is the many everyday little things which make our life here so joyful. We find one of the best ways to improve our French is to ask friends to eat with us when I can also demonstrate that the English have good food too.

This testimony from our student Marion Stonehouse demonstrates, among many other things, how life in France can be enjoyable. She acknowledges, as well, some of the negative aspects of the country, the need to be patient with the French bureaucracy, the long summer holidays when everything is closed and when "it is best to avoid being ill," and the way the French drivers behave on the road:

> We cannot understand why charming French people become Attila the Hun once behind the steering wheel of their car. We have adapted our approach to driving to accommodate and so far continue to survive. [...]
>
> And what about the language? It is not an insurmountable problem unless you choose to make it one. Our desire to participate as fully as possible in the French way of life has been our chief incentive. We listen to what is going on around us, we watch only French TV, I go to a craft class where no-one speaks English. You have to be brave and jump in! Your efforts

are appreciated. Each contact brings a small success, a little more understanding and we build on this.

Another student, Carolyn, who lives in the Languedoc Roussillon region, goes further on the question of language:

> The best way to learn French is to 'be French'. Try not to compare how things are done in England or in your own country. Remember that it was your choice to move and accept that life is different. To begin with, watch French television. At first it will be hard, but the news is the same in any language. Games shows are good because the language is repetitive. If you watch them regularly you will hear certain expressions repeated time and time again. Talk back and practice. Buy magazines with lots of pictures and absorb the language. Try not to translate word for word but grasp the general meaning. Be observant, watch mannerisms and facial expressions, listen to the intonation. For example, when you are shopping or in a café eavesdrop on conversations. Make friends with your neighbors, they are a mine of useful information, be patient and eventually you will understand what they are trying to tell you!

Sue, a British student, also told us: "The French are patient, kind people generally and will not snigger at your strange grammar or funny accent. They really just appreciate you making an effort." The same with James and Elma:

> Contrary to the widely held opinion amongst many English people, we have experienced nothing but kindness and polite-

ness since moving. It is very pleasant to be able to walk without the fear of experiencing yobbish behavior and litter strewn streets. If you are thinking of moving to France, do not hesitate, do move! As long as you realize that you cannot create a Little England in your adopted country, then you will experience a new way of life and find that your former closest neighbors geographically can become your closest neighbors and friends in your new house, wherever you decide to live in France. Yes, we have had some problems, but nothing that could not be resolved by our new French friends. Incidentally, we have shared evenings when we speak only in French or in English, which helps us all.

Even in Paris, where life is much more frenzied than in the quiet provinces of France, the life of an expat can be very pleasant. This is what Debbie, who bought a studio in Paris, told us:

I like the rhythm of French life — the ritual of the greetings when you enter and leave a store, meals at fixed times, everyone watching the news at 8:00 pm, no shopping on Sundays —

> *I like the rhythm of French life — the ritual of the greetings when you enter and leave a store, meals at fixed times, everyone watching the news at 8:00 pm, no shopping on Sundays... Even the strikes don't bother me...*
> Debbie, a student of Learn French at Home

compared to the hectic pace of my normal routine. Even the strikes don't bother me. So what if the *métro* doesn't run for a day or two? It means no wait at the Laundromat — everyone will be busy marching!

A few amusing or surprising anecdotes

Among the hundreds of testimonies we receive from our students, some anecdotes they tell us are quite amusing. Like the one by Diane, who lives in the Brittany region:

> We made every effort to integrate; we never turned down any invitations even if we were unsure what was expected of us. We went with big smiles, good firm handshakes introducing ourselves '*oui*' and '*non*' in hopefully all the right places. One of my first gaffs was when I was trying to explain that 'I had fed the dog' belonging to a very old *paysanne* who had been taken to hospital. I apparently was telling everyone 'I had eaten the dog.' Lucky for me my French friends realized what I was trying to say. But they were proud, not only that I was feeding the dog but also trying to speak their language.

Equally interesting, and rather surprising, is the remark made by an English student, Elisabeth Ashley, during an interview which took place in Paris, and where she presented a slightly different idea than the normal image people have of French men. At the question: "French men have the reputation for being rather macho. Have you noticed any differences, compared to other parts of the world, in how you are treated as a single woman both as you walk through the streets and also in restaurants, cafés, etc.," she replied:

I find French men hilarious out on the streets of Paris. They are quite different from British men. British men tend to shout out of vans at girls if they are going to comment at all in the street. Here a French man will mutter something complimentary almost under his breath to a woman as they pass each other in the street. Much more polite!

Les bises (kisses on the cheek)

Talking of politeness, an aspect of the French way of relating to each other that scares most foreigners is to kiss each other on the cheek. If you travel to France only for a few days, this is not of direct interest to you, unless you meet some friends or their family, but if you intend to settle in France, there is no doubt that you will have to deal with it!

Each time you run into someone you know, a friend or even simply an acquaintance, a neighbor, a member of a family who has invited you for dinner, or the parents of friends of your children, you should be prepared to give from two to four *bises*, depending on your location in France. This may happen even if you are meeting that person for the first time (of course, this does not apply if this person is a storekeeper or a waiter...), and to people with whom you are not close enough to say "*tu*."

The same applies when you say good bye to this person. If you stay at a friend's house for a few days, or for a long time, you should expect to exchange kisses every morning and evening. It is the same at work, in most cases, with your colleagues, and at school, or college.

It differs if you are a man or a woman. French men usually do not kiss each other except if they are very close friends or family members. If you are a man, you should only be ready to *faire la bise* to a woman, but normally you would shake hands (*serrer la main*) with another man. If you are a woman, you are supposed to kiss both men and women. Women can also shake hands but this is much more formal. When you have an appointment with a banker or a doctor, they will automatically take the initiative of shaking hands with you. In any case, as you are a foreigner, the French person will more likely initiate the action of kissing you, understanding that you may not be fully aware of the procedure to follow. The tricky part is to know how many *bises* you should give.

Even the French are confused with that. In Paris, it is either two or four. In most of the north, in a wide circle from the Loire region, the Atlantic Ocean, and all around Paris, it is four. In Brittany, it used to be only one but a new trend is to double this figure, while in most of the east and south-west of France it is two, and in the south of the *Massif central* and part of Provence, it is three. In a small part of Corsica it can go up to five.

You should not worry, though, if you do not pick the right number, the French make that mistake all the time, which results in comments such as: "Oh yes, I forgot it is four here, in my family in the south, it is three, and at work it is two..." In case of doubt, always start with two, and wait to see what the other person does. If you are an American and are used to giving big hugs, avoid doing that to French men or women unless you know them well enough and you can tell them that it is something you do in your country, or if they are used to it already. A woman who is not used to it might find it very unpleasant.

> *If you stay at a friend's house for a few days, or for a long time, you should expect to exchange kisses every morning and evening. It is the same at work, in most cases, with your colleagues, and at school, or college.*

Moving to another country is not moving to "Utopia"

This is what our English student, Shelley Rudock, who moved to the South-West of France a few years ago, told us:

> I think ultimately moving to another country is not moving to Utopia, and we should never fool ourselves that it is. You tend to swap one set of problems for another different set, since life is a rollercoaster wherever you live. If you accept that there can be huge benefits to living in France, and that some things may be more difficult or frustrating, then you are more likely to settle in more comfortably.

Peta Matthews, another British woman who settled in Normandy, added something which everyone who becomes an expatriate in a country should be aware of: "As a foreigner, I don't think one ever entirely integrates; and I think that part of the challenge is accepting that situation and feeling comfortable with it. After all, one is never going to be French... I only watch French TV but my husband does like English programs." Asked if she and her husband have acquired any new habits since they have been living in Normandy, she replied:

> Yes — we never, ever drink instant coffee now, only ground. We eat more bread with meals; we are more discerning about food; we take more time discussing things; we go to the beach regularly; we spend more time outside in the garden; we go to the Saturday market; my husband uses the airport more; we enjoy a *kir* as an *apéro*; we go to bed much later than in England. We read more.

She ends by giving some very intelligent advice to anyone who is contemplating moving to France: "Learn the language to the best of your ability and keep trying to improve. Be flexible about events. Give things time — nothing is ever perfect to begin with."

That being said, let us just end this chapter with comments made by other people than our students, expressing warmly how they love their life in France: "The sweetness and generosity and politeness and gentleness and humanity of the French had shown me how lovely life can be if one takes time to be friendly," wrote the famous American chef and author Julia Child in *My Life in France*. "I just love France, I love French people, I love the French language, I love French food. I love their mentality. I just feel like it's me. I'm very French," also said, on a very enthusiastic note, the French actress and model of Ukrainian origin Olga Kurylenko in an interview for CraveOnline, in 2008.

> *The sweetness and generosity and politeness and gentleness and humanity of the French had shown me how lovely life can be if one takes time to be friendly.*
> Julia Child, chef and writer

TO REMEMBER FROM CHAPTER 25

• When you enter a store or a bus, when you ask people in the street for directions, **always start with** *Bonjour!*

• Try to speak like the French. Listen to conversations between French people, and see how the people react when you speak, and do not hesitate to ask them if what you have said is correct.

• **Be prepared for frank remarks and some rudeness...** and **do not make a big deal** about it.

• Did you know that **France is considered to be the best country in the world by many students?** Read their **testimonies, and those of foreigners who have chosen to settle in France** — with a few amusing anecdotes.

• **Learn how to kiss French people on the cheek...**

• Remember: **Moving to another country is not moving to** "Utopia".

26. TIME TO SHARE YOUR KNOWLEDGE: FRENCH LESSONS FOR CHILDREN

SINCE JIM BECAME THE GRAND-FATHER of a little girl, Soraya, in 2011, he has adopted the habit of speaking in French to her from time to time, of teaching her a few French words, which she loves repeating. They listen to and sing French songs together, and read children's stories in French. He is amazed to see how quickly she learns, and how much she loves speaking French! For her 4th Birthday, she received a new book in French for children, by Eugene Ionesco, that they started reading together. When Jim visited her a few weeks after, she told him that she wanted him to read a book to her. He was surprised that she picked this one among so many other children's books.

It is a very well known fact that children are like sponges with languages, learning so fast that this can be challenging for their parents who cannot always keep up with them. Children can also quickly acquire the right accent. Studies have shown that learning one or several languages is excellent for their development, and definitely positive for their future whatever they choose to do when they get older. Therefore, we can only encourage parents to give their children the opportunity to learn a second language, and not just in school. In this chapter, we will limit ourselves to recall the basics of second language acquisition for children, but we could devote a full book to the question.

To be bilingual: a wonderful asset for the future

What we have noted in this book about all the advantages that you can gain by being bilingual is even more so the case for children. In an article published in *Parents Magazine*, a journalist, Ilisa Cohen, asked: "Why are so many families jumping on the bilingual bandwagon?" Nancy Rhodes, director of foreign-language education at the Center for Applied Linguistics, in Washington, D.C. answers that question: "In our increasingly global world, parents realize that their kids will benefit from knowing more than one language. There's definitely been a grassroots push for more bilingual education in preschools." Ilisa Cohen continues: "Exposing your child to a second language will help him learn about other cultures. Research has shown that bilinguals tend to be more creative thinkers than those who speak one language, and one study suggests that their brain functions may stay sharper as they age."

Several other authors confirm how beneficial it is for children to be bilingual or multilingual. "Learning another language actually enhances a child's overall verbal development," Roberta Michnick Golinkoff, Ph.D., and Kathy Hirsh-Pasekin, in *How Babies Talk*, said. Several scientific studies have confirmed that it also develops their analytical abilities, cognitive flexibility and other skills.

> *Exposing your child to a second language will help him learn about other cultures. Research has shown that bilinguals tend to be more creative thinkers than those who speak one language.*
> Ilisa Cohen, journalist

It the Opinion section of *The New York Times*, on March 11th, 2016, entitled *The Superior Social Skills of Bilinguals,* Katherine Kinzler, associate professor of psychology and human development at Cornell University, who conducted studies on children ages 4-6 and on babies of 14 to 16 months, explained:

> Being bilingual has some obvious advantages. Learning more than one language enables new conversations and new experiences. But in recent years, psychology researchers have demonstrated some less obvious advantages of bilingualism, too. For example, bilingual children may enjoy certain cognitive benefits, such as improved executive function — which is critical for problem solving and other mentally demanding activities.
>
> Now, two new studies demonstrate that multilingual exposure improves not only children's cognitive skills but also their social abilities.
>
> One study from my development psychology lab [...] shows that multilingual children can be better at communication than monolingual children. [...]
>
> Interestingly, we also found that children who were effectively monolingual yet regularly exposed to another language — for example, those who had grandparents who spoke another language — were just as talented as the bilingual children. [...]
>
> ...the social advantage we have identified appears to emerge from merely being raised in an environment in which multiple languages are experienced, not from being bilingual per se. This is potentially good news for parents who are not bilingual

themselves, yet who want their children to enjoy some of the benefits of multilingualism.

Equally important, learning a second language does not interfere with learning their native language properly. Many reports have specifically demonstrated that children who have learned a second language earn higher SAT scores, particularly on the verbal section of the test.

We should also point out that people who are being interviewed for a job and who possess more than one language will find it much easier, whatever profession they might choose, to be selected from among candidates who master only their native language. This may have a major impact on their career, and on their whole life.

At what age to start?

There is no definite rule, no specific age, and it is never too late to start. Many specialists would say that the earlier the better. For children who start very early, between 2 to 3 years old, the second language may immediately become second nature. "They are developing language skills rapidly, and they quickly absorb whatever they hear," explained Erika Levy, Ph.D., assistant professor of speech and language pathology at Columbia University, in the same article published in *Parents Magazine* cited above. "They can learn to understand

> *Multilingual exposure improves not only children's cognitive skills but also their social abilities.*
> Katherine Kinzler, associate professor of psychology and human development at Cornell University

new words in two different languages at an incredibly fast rate." Ilisa Cohen added: "Two- and 3-year-olds are not only increasing their vocabularies, they're starting to recognize the speech patterns they've been hearing since birth. The earlier you introduce a second language, the easier it will be for your child to pick up its unique sounds."

However, we know from experience that even if they start a little later, between 6 to 12, they can still, depending on the situation, the reasons for choosing a language and the motivation, absorb a new language extremely quickly and even become totally bilingual. And if they start learning before the onset of adolescence, they are much more likely to acquire native-like pronunciation. The best situation is, of course, when the family moves to a foreign country, even only for a few months, and when the child follows the curriculum of the country, i.e., studying in the local language. To be fully immersed in the language at school is also the best way to get the right accent. We have observed quite often among our students — and from the personal experience of several of our teachers — that children who move to France with their family and start French school, even if they speak their native language at home, can learn to speak French very quickly, as early as three months after their arrival. After a few more months, French people who do not know them may even think they are French natives.

What method to choose?

The choice of the teaching method is very important. In an article published by PBS Parents, *Ways to Introduce Your Kids to Foreign Languages*, Grace Hwang Lynch talked about her own experience, which was not so positive:

> As the daughter of immigrants from Taiwan, I wanted to share the Chinese language with my kids. So when my older son reached kindergarten, I signed him up for Chinese school. Af-

ter a few years, the weekly two-hour classes — plus homework — took a toll on our family. And my son still couldn't speak Chinese!

Then, she provided some information on the most popular methods used to help the parents find the right way for their child to learn another language, such as bilingual immersion, i.e.: Learning a second language is integrated with the academic curriculum. "This teaches them a second language the way they learn their first language," Nancy Rhodes, cited in this article, commented. However, such programs are far from being available in all school districts.

Grace Hwang Lynch also mentioned extracurricular programs taking place on weekends. However, "sometimes kids can feel too mentally drained after a full week of school to spend yet another day in a classroom." Finally, she presented the fact that parents who are fluent in a foreign language and who speak to their children in that language represents a method which usually works extremely well.

She quoted a native of Finland, Iria Nishimura, who said: "Speaking another language at home was like eating or sleeping, part of our home life. Nothing to it. The kids have never commented to me if learning Finnish was hard or not." Finally, she suggested

> *Speaking another language at home was like eating or sleeping, part of our home life.*
> Iria Nishimura, parent of a bilingual child

that travelling to a foreign country would give children the chance to "experience other languages and cultures," and she insisted on the importance of, whatever method is chosen, to make it fun — which, we fully agree, is definitely fundamental.

She added: "Of course, a child won't learn to speak another language fluently from hearing words, watching videos, or singing songs. But simply being exposed to a language" will help him/her understand phrases when he/she hears them. "So even though you probably won't be having a French conversation with your child very soon, if you say '*bonne nuit*' every night at bedtime," the child will "figure out what you mean."

Learning by Skype? The children love it — and it works!

Your children may have many different ways of learning French, either at school or while travelling, or with bilingual family members. However, many of them do not have so many opportunities and may very well, like Grace Hwang Lynch's son, fail at learning as quickly as the parents hope. Making the children work overtime to learn a language is not always very well received and does not prove very productive, unless they are extremely motivated. It is also time consuming for the parents, and may take on the time devoted to sports or cultural activities that are also very important for the children. Not very many schools offer excellent opportunities for learning other languages, and the specialized schools are not always easily accessible.

This is why, as early as 2007, after we realized the need, we created a special program of children's lessons via Skype that was designed for children from 6 to 12 years of age. We were able to quickly confirm that children learn very fast and are generally attracted and motivated to learn if the lesson is performed in a relaxed and fun atmosphere.

Equally rapidly, we could witness how they found taking their lesson via Skype exciting — mainly because kids love to use the computer and appreciate the real time interaction!

The lessons last only 30 to 45 minutes, but with a pair of earphones, a webcam and some visual teaching material, the children do not see the time pass. The teacher targets the lesson's objective towards comprehension. Through games, pictures, drawings, small role plays, songs and more, he/she keeps the student's attention during the entire lesson. Immediately afterwards, the child receives by email the vocabulary taught during the lesson as well as one or two exercises to do as homework. The lessons can be taken on a weekday or on a weekend at any suitable time for the child, who feels very comfortable taking them in his/her room, surrounded by his/her own books, toys and stuffed animals.

Sometimes, it happens that the mother or the father joins the child during the lesson, offering his/her help or because they are simply curious to see how it goes. However, several parents told us that their child makes them understand immediately that they are not welcome. They say: "Mom, please, we are working!" And then, when it is time for the next lesson, the child goes to his/her room and, before closing the door, tells the parents: "See you later! Now it's time for my lesson with MY French teacher." Once, before signing up for a series of lessons for his daughter, a father living on the west coast of the USA asked us: "Please, my son wants a French native teacher living in France, it makes it more unique for him to have a teacher who is living so far from home."

> *Once, before signing up for a series of lessons for his daughter, a father living in the USA asked us: "Please, my son wants a French native teacher living in France, it makes it more unique for him to have a teacher who is living so far from home."*

Since its creation, the children's lessons with Skype have been one of our most successful programs. Apart from teaching a second language to children who have no access to foreign language lessons at school or close to their home, it is also very much used by parents who are homeschooling. Now, many children who are being homeschooled are learning French through our program.

Among the many comments we receive from parents is the following one by Nicola Christinger-Grant, a former journalist for the BBC and other media outlets who moved to Zurich, Switzerland, where she ran her own English pre-school for a few years, and who is the author of the children's book *The Fish with a Wish: and other stories*. She explained how and why she enrolled her daughter Victoria in our French lessons program, and her reactions nine weeks after they began:

> By chance, a contact in France introduced me to *Learn French at Home*... I was intrigued by what the company was offering and their language-learning methods, so I decided to sign Victoria up. It was simple preparation; I enrolled her via their website and talked to Céline about our move and what I hoped Victoria would gain from the lessons. [...]
>
> Victoria's teacher is a wonderful lady, she is sensitive and encouraging, and since Victoria started nine weeks ago her confidence is at an all-time high. She now looks forward to every Wednesday; she gets an immediate benefit by not only intensive listening and speaking but also seeing the language written on the computer in front of her. She is totally relaxed, and like most 12- year olds, is very comfortable with the computer and the 45-minute lesson passes by in a flash.

When living in France, how do the children adapt?

All the testimonies we receive from expatriates in France with children are similar: The children adapt very well, and often much easier and faster than the parents. For example, our English student, Seona Reilly, recounted:

> I have two boys ages 7 and 8. They were 4 and 6 when we moved here. My eldest son adapted very quickly and speaks French well now, which is useful when I get stuck! My youngest had a hard time in the bilingual system, learning in French one day and English the next, but since changing to a French school his French has improved considerably.

Then, quite often, comes a stage when the child knows more than his parents and starts making them feel embarrassed. When one of our American students, E., a mother of two children who had moved to French-speaking Switzerland, started her lessons by Skype with *Learn French at Home*, her main motivation was to be able to cope with her children's knowledge. Not only she wanted to be able to help them with their homework, and to communicate easily with their teachers and other parents, but she confessed to us that she wanted to improve her own spoken language as, on several occasions, she had been embarrassed by the reactions of her children who were ashamed of her poor French.

In an op-ed for *The New York times*, Pamela Druckerman wrote:

> Earlier this year, I took my kids to see a soccer match in Paris. Along with practically everyone else in the stands, we chanted *Allez les Bleus* — Go Blues — to cheer on the French team. But a few minutes into the game, my 6-year-old started to look uncomfortable. 'Mommy, it's not *les blooes*, it's *les bleuh*,' he whis-

pered. Immigrant parents famously embarrass their kids... As an American expatriate whose kids were born in France, I'm an expert on this subject. When you're the foreigner and your kids are the natives, they realize you're clueless much sooner than they ordinarily would.

She even questions her own attitude in a few situations, for example this one, which is a good example of the challenge that parents can sometimes meet:

> Am I so cowed by my kids (or by the local culture) that I'm not defending their interests? I suspect this issue is especially acute in France, a country where 'discreet' is high praise, and people live by the motto, 'to be happy, be hidden.' An ex-Chicagoan who lives in Paris told me that her daughters beg her 'not to do a revolution' whenever she wants to speak to a teacher about problems at school. It's unclear whether a revolution would even help. But to save them from embarrassment, she said, 'I make a concerted effort not to do a revolution' except in extreme cases...

This is just one aspect of being bilingual for an expatriate child. There are many others, explained Pamela Druckerman. For example: "It's becoming clear that being bilingual is more than just a party trick or a neutral skill." As the French level of her daughter improves, she added:

> She's starting to bring home not just unfamiliar expressions but also new ideas and rules. Her new language is making her into not just a French speaker but into a French person." By the

spring of her first year in *maternelle*, "friends tell me that her American twang is gone. She sounds like a genuine *Parisienne*. She's become so confident in French that I overhear her joking around with friends, in French, in an exaggerated American accent..."

> *By the spring of her first year in* maternelle, *friends tell me that her American twang is gone. She sounds like a genuine* Parisienne.
> Pamela Druckerman, journalist and writer

TO REMEMBER FROM CHAPTER 26

- **Children absorb foreign languages like sponges**, learning so fast that **this can be challenging for their parents** who cannot always keep up with them!

- **To be bilingual will be a wonderful asset for their future.**

- **At what age to start?** There is **no definite rule, no specific age**, and **it is never too late to start**.

- **The choice of the best method is very important**, but not always easy. **Read what a few parents have to say about it.**

- **Children love taking lessons by Skype** with a teacher who is in France, and **it works! They even make wonderful progress** through this way of teaching.

- **When living in France, children adapt amazingly well** — which may create **another challenge for their parents**...

27. IN CONCLUSION: HAS BECOMING FLUENT IN FRENCH CHANGED YOU?

THE DAY YOU ARE ABLE to acknowledge that you have finally achieved your dream, being fluent in French, it will be time to reflect, not only on the magic process that led you from knowing no French at all and to being fluent, but on how this has changed you. You will be amazed by what you will discover.

Re-discovering your own language

"By learning a new language I discover mine, I analyze it more, I understand much better my own grammar," said the Canadian novelist Nancy Huston, whose mother tongue is English but who writes primarily in French. When she does write in English, she translates it herself into French.

This is the first sign that learning French will have changed you: Speaking English will not be as natural as it was before, or at least you will notice constantly what can seem bizarre in your language, by comparison with what is very strange in French.

Akira Mizubayashi, who is totally bilingual Japanese-English, goes on quoting Nancy Huston: "The acquisition of a second language interferes with the natural character of the native language — from there, nothing is obvious, neither in one of the languages nor in the other; nothing from the original language belongs to you."

He added, referring to himself: "The day I took possession of the French language, I actually lost forever Japanese in its original purity. My native language lost its status as a first language. I learned to speak like a foreigner in my own language." He ended by saying that he always feels out of place," but that this is a wonderful way to "express all my love for the French language, all my fondness for Japanese."

This aspect of re-discovering one's own language while learning French is well-known by our advanced students. It happens constantly with Jim during his French lessons. He says: "Ah, the French say this in such a way? Why? This is so strange... But in fact we have something quite similar in English, I hadn't realized before..." And we continue discussing an English expression or a grammar point before going back to French.

The Canadian entrepreneur and writer Scott H. Young, quoted in a previous chapter, confirms: "One unexpected benefit of learning French is how much it has taught me about the way I speak English. Nothing shines a light on how we speak like going back to the beginning and starting over again."

It is interesting to note that those who are studying French are not the only ones to make this same assessment. Their teachers share exactly, and constantly, the same experience. For example, each time

> *One unexpected benefit of learning French is how much it has taught me about the way I speak English. Nothing shines a light on how we speak like going back to the beginning and starting over again.*
> Scott H. Young, entrepreneur and writer

a student seems surprised or starts laughing when learning a new idiomatic expression or a new way of expressing a feeling, the teacher, who is used to these expressions in his/her own native language, realizes how strange it is and wonders where it comes from. This is an excellent matter for discussion with the students. Very often, having an etymologic dictionary at hand is very useful!

You know you're becoming more French when...

Julia Greenhalf, a Melbourne based correspondent, editor, blogger and language lover, goes further in a post in the online magazine *My French Life*™, entitled: *You know you're becoming more French when...* She follows with a long enumeration of how you may have changed. This is said with humor, of course, but there is a lot of truth in what she says.

Here are a few of the more characteristic differences she has listed:
—You say "*bonjour*" and "*au revoir*" to everyone, including the bus driver.
—You stop hugging and understand the importance of multiple cheek kisses.
—You know that if you want something from someone, you'll start your query with "*excusez-moi*."
—You consider bread a utensil to eat with other foods.
—You need cheese like it's oxygen.
—You don't bat an eye when there's yet another (métro) strike.
—You know French slang or *verlan* (the trend of reversing the syllables of some words).
—You find yourself swearing more. And it carries across into your English.
—You drop *mots d'anglais* into your sentences with a French accent.
—You know that the word *terrible* is a slippery slope.
—You know an acceptable response to a question is a shrug and "*bof*" with pursed lips. You can have a whole conversation in French without saying a word.
—You think calling someone a flea or a cabbage is cute.

When you realize that you have become a rather different person

The fact is that, after a few years, you may discover that there is now something French in you. But there is more: Being fluent in another language makes you a distinctly different person.

"What you get by achieving your goals is not as important as what you become by achieving your goals," the German writer and statesman Johann Wolfgang Von Goethe said.

When we ask our students who have reached a very good level of French how their study may have changed them, most of them say that they now feel quite different. Shinji, our Japanese student who speaks both English and French fluently, even told us:

> I have changed so much since I started speaking French! I have another view on many things and attitudes. I think I have learned to become more tolerant and accepting, more open to new opinions. Also, before, I thought that the Western culture was the same everywhere, now I am able to better understand the differences between the French, the Americans, the English, the German, etc. Now, there is even something of a Westerner in me, in the way I analyze some facts and situations.

> *I have changed so much since I started speaking French! I have another view on many things and attitudes. I think I have learned to become more tolerant and accepting, more open to new opinions.*
> Shinji, a student of *Learn French at Home*

Judith Meyer, a young German woman who has a passion for languages, writes a very interesting blog (LearnLangs.com). One of her posts, *13 Ways Language-learning Changes How You Think*, confirmed all we have said above, and adds that knowing a new language makes it "easier to remain rational" and also "to remain emotionally detached," among many other changes in your way of thinking.

Several studies, that have been conducted on bilinguals, also show that many people can change their attitude depending on which language they express themselves in. In a blog published in 2013 (in TechValleyConnect.com), Jenna Brydges, a scholar who lived in China and speaks fluent mandarin, wrote a post entitled *Be Prepared For a New Personality When You Learn a New Language*. In this article, she confirmed that "research has shown that those who have acquired skills in a second language often feel they have acquired a second personality along with it." After having noticed this personality switch in some of her classmates, she "decided to ask thousands of former exchange students whether or not they have had similar experiences." She "was immediately bombarded by a deluge of responses from foreign language speakers from around the world."

> *Several studies, that have been conducted on bilinguals, show that many people can change their attitude depending on which language they express themselves in.*

Here are some of them:
—"Totally! My native language is Spanish, and when I speak English I don't change that much. But when I switch to Japanese, even my body language is different, it's like I'm someone else!"
—"I totally do that. In English I'm mostly in control, but sometimes anxious. In Spanish I'm light-hearted and joking, and in German I'm either stony or silly. I think German has more to do with ability than anything else though."

—"I'm an English native-speaker and know Italian and Spanish... I don't notice much change when I speak Spanish, but I definitely have different inflection and even slightly different humor when I'm speaking Italian... and while I rarely use my hands when speaking English, there's no way to speak Italian without the gestures..."

Jenna Brydges concludes: "Body movements, hand gestures, facial expressions — even your sense of humor can change with the switch of a language."

Speaking a new language has many amazing side benefits, and not only with regard to the small habits or gestures mentioned above. It is almost as if you have started to lead a double life.

Once, while Nancy Huston was hesitating about whether to start her new novel in English or in French, she wrote an email to her friend, the South-African writer André Brink, who also writes in two languages, asking him for advice. He replied: "Don't worry, just start, I often do that: I write a chapter in the language in which it comes more naturally, and I translate later." She adds: "He was very relaxed about it. He told me that we are lucky, compared to the others, to live twice."

Many authors have also emphasized how knowing a new language can change your life. For example, Frank Smith, a well-known and respected English psycholinguist and author of many books, who said: "One language sets you in a corridor of life. Two languages open every door along the way."

The German entrepreneur Karl Albrecht had another way to express it: "Change your language and you change your thoughts."

> *One language sets you in a corridor f life. Two languages open every door along the way.*
> Frank Smith, psycholinguist and author

This is confirmed by the renowned journalist of *The New York Times* Flora Lewis, who travelled worldwide and had many occasions to appreciate that knowing a new language can increase your capacity for feeling, or understanding what is happening around you: "Learning another language is not only learning different words for the same things, but learning another way to think about things."

A Czech proverb goes further: "You live a new life for every new language you speak. If you know only one language, you live only once."

Improving your French might turn out to be a life-long project

"Learning French is not a matter of a few years... It is, on the contrary, an implausible, haunting, gigantic project that involves a whole life." If the way Akira Mizubayashi views his learning of the French language is a little extreme, the truth is that, even if you consider yourself fully fluent, if you have fulfilled your goal or even gone beyond, you will always have something to double check, to discover, to learn, to be surprised about. To do so means, of course, that you are still interested, or at least curious about some aspects of French that remain a mystery — or annoyed to realize that you still make mistakes. In such a case, you may just feel like Mizubayashi: "Spelling, vocabulary, or grammar mistakes, we of course make them, and we will never be totally free of that. Therefore, we will always have a few very well chosen dictionaries as our companions, as if they were the best friends in the world and that will never leave us."

Without being obsessed by it, Jim shares this feeling, as do some of our students. Learning always a little more, unveiling the best hidden secrets of the French language, has become a permanent engagement, as well as a joy.

The French language is undeniably complex. From time to time, French intellectuals and government officials discuss the possibility of simplify it in view of reinforcing the assimilation of the vocabulary and the grammar by young people who find it so difficult and make many mistakes. Interviewed by a journalist about such attempts, the French writer Philippe Delerm, who was a teacher of French in junior high school for thirty-three years, replied:

> It is not by creating a ready-made frame of logic to limit the language, or by betting on a 'cheaper' and weaker language which would seem easier... that we will help people learn it. It is by giving them a taste for the French language, by practicing it and showing the language in all its magic that we can help them. We are fortunate enough to have a language which is extremely illogical, subtle, paradoxical, too, and this is what comprises its richness.

As Jean-Louis Boutefou pointed out in the editorial we quoted at the beginning of this book, becoming fluent in French will present you with a long list of challenges, but will also provide you with countless rewards, and will give you access to the fine points of

---

We are fortunate enough to have a language which is extremely illogical, subtle, paradoxical, too, and this is what comprises its richness.
Philippe Delerm, former teacher and writer

French culture. And even after you have reached a level at which you are supposed to be very comfortable, you may still want to know or understand more. Learning French can definitely be a lifelong project.

This is what has become the case for Jim, who will never want to stop learning but will certainly always be eager to know more, to continue trying to decipher one of the frequent puns in *Le Canard enchaîné*, to listen to French podcasts as often as he can, to follow closely the French news, to speak with French people, and to enjoy fully each of his trips to France. And while he may never become totally French, he will undoubtedly continue to evolve as a person, and eventually enter the realm of living twice.

> *While he may never become totally French, Jim will undoubtedly continue to evolve as a person, and eventually enter the realm of living twice.*

TO REMEMBER FROM CHAPTER 27

- **By learning French, you will re-discover your own language.**

- **You may also realize that you have become a rather different person:** More tolerant and accepting? more ready to accept changes? remaining more rational and less emotional?... These are a few changes you may notice. And also the interesting and surprising fact that **you will behave and act differently according to the language you are speaking.**

- You may even notice, through a few changes, that **you have become "more French!"**

- For some of you, a new language might even mean a new life... and **becoming totally fluent a life-long project!** There are abundant testimonials of that metamorphosis.

ANNEX: A FEW USEFUL RESOURCES

The selection listed below is far from exhaustive, but it mainly consists of the websites that Jim and other students find useful in their daily practice. We can only advise every French learner to take advantage as much as possible of such tools that are accessible online. They can help them improve their knowledge, and they are also an excellent window into French culture.

1. Online dictionaries
—**Word Reference** — free and multilingual, with verb conjugations and a reader's forum which can be very useful in finding good translations of difficult expressions:
www.wordreference.com
—**Ultralingua** — also multilingual, not free but very useful, especially as it can be downloaded on any device, including smartphones:
www.ultralingua.com/products/french-english-dictionary.html
—**Collins** — an excellent dictionary:
www.collinsdictionary.com/dictionary/english-french

2. General learning and grammar websites
Duolingo — A French free learning program that is very popular among our students. You just need to register. You can also download it on your smartphone: www.duolingo.com

Other sites:
www.tolearnfrench.com
http://french.about.com
www.laits.utexas.edu/tex
www.bonjourdefrance.com/index/indexgram.htm
https://apps.carleton.edu/curricular/fren/Language_tools
www.polarfle.com

3. Tools for French verb conjugation
www.verbix.com
http://leconjugueur.lefigaro.fr/php5/index.php?verbe
www.laits.utexas.edu/tex/gr/tap10.html
http://mnaatf.org/Bonnesidees/BonnesIdeesLBelatecheSum08.pdf

4. Vocabulary and idiomatic expressions
www.languageguide.org/french/
http://lexiquefle.free.fr
www.digitaldialects.com/French.htm
www.expressio.fr
http://doyouspeaktouriste.fr/#&panel1-1

5. Podcasts

Free French podcasts about various topics:

www.french-podcasts.com
www.podcastfrancaisfacile.com

Radio programs:

Radio France: *La marche de l'Histoire*
http://radiofrance-podcast.net/podcast09/rss_11739.xml
Radio France Internationale (RFI):
—*Une semaine d'actualité*
www1.rfi.fr/radiofr/podcast/Podcast_SEM.asp

—*Idées*
http://www.rfi.fr/emission/idees/podcast
—*La danse des mots*
http://www1.rfi.fr/radiofr/podcast/Podcast_DANSE.xml
France Inter:
—*Là-bas si j'y suis*
http://direct-radio.fr/France-Inter/Podcast/Daniel-Mermet/La-bas-si-j-y-suis
—*Sur les épaules de Darwin*
http://direct-radio.fr/cat/podcasts/podcast-radio/sur-les-%C3%A9paules-de-darwin
Radio Monte Carlo (RMC): *Bourdin & Co*
http://direct-radio.fr/RMC/podcast/Jean-Jacques-Bourdin/Bourdin-and-CO

6. Videos
—**BBC:**
www.bbc.co.uk/languages/french
—**TV5 Monde:**
http://parlons-francais.tv5monde.com/webdocumentaires-pour-apprendre-le-francais/p-1-lg0-Accueil.htm
—**TV7:**
www.tv7.com
—**Radio Télévision suisse (RTS):**
www.rts.ch

7. Song lyrics

Here is a selection of websites that present many song lyrics in French:

—**Paroles.net:**
www.paroles.net
—**ParolesMania:**
www.parolesmania.com

—**Wiki Paroles:**
http://fr.lyrics.wikia.com/wiki/WikiaParoles

8. Articles from the media to read online

Most French newspapers have a selection of articles that are accessible online without subscription and are an excellent source of reading material. Here are just a few examples:

—*Le Monde*
www.lemonde.fr
—*Libération*
www.liberation.fr
—*Radio France Internationale* **(RFI)** - the radio also publishes on its website short news articles to read:
www.rfi.fr
—*Courrier International*
www.courrierinternational.com

9. A selection of accessible books

Our students regularly ask our advice about books that are not too difficult and that they could try reading. They also exchange names of authors and titles of books that they had liked on our online Forum.

Books for children: There are many books we can recommend. Particularly the series of stories of *Le Petit Nicolas*, that are quite easy, charming, of very good quality of writing by an excellent author, René Goscinny, nicely illustrated by one of the most famous French artists, Jean-Jacques Sempé.

A few francophone writers: Among the contemporary novelists that French students find not too difficult to read are:

—**Marc Lévy**, who publishes a book every year, always a bestseller.
—**Amélie Nothomb**, who is Belgian but lives in Paris. Every one of the books she publishes every year is also a bestseller. They also have the advantage of being very short.
—**Guillaume Musso**, who is also among the authors who sells the most books in France. He publishes a new novel almost every year.
—**Tatiana de Rosnay**, who is another very popular French novelist, publishes many novels but also short stories which are even easier to read.
—**Aki Shimazaki**, a Japanese author who lives in Canada and writes in French. Her series of five short novels, *Le Poids des secrets*, is very easy to read, and is both moving and captivating.

There are many more, of course... A suggestion: If you are not sure that you will fully understand a book written in French, find a copy of the English translation (or in any other language depending on your native tongue) and compare it to the original each time you cannot understand a paragraph.

10. Learning tools for children

There is a multitude of websites of teaching material for children. The ones we recommend the most are those that make the children learn through games and songs.

Games and exercises:
www.ortholud.com
www.jeuxdememoire.net
www.education.vic.gov.au/LanguagesOnline/french/french.htm
www.tolearnfrench.com — this website that we also recommended above has many funny exercises for children.

Children's songs:
http://comptines.tv
www.mondedestitounis.fr/chanson-enfant.php

ACKNOWLEDGEMENTS

We especially wish to thank Jim Merical, whose example served as the common thread of this book.

We also thank all the members of the online Forum of *Learn French at Home*, whose replies to the *Question du Jour* have been useful as examples of the feelings expressed by many of our students.

We also thank all the students of *Learn French at Home* who have given us a written testimony and recommendations after having taken lessons with the teachers of our school.

Of course, we also thank all the teachers of *Learn French at Home*, for their professionalism, their devotion and their patience, who are rightly and highly appreciated by all our students.

REFERENCES

I - BOOKS

Akita, Lailah Gifty. *The Alphabets of Success — Passion Driven Life*. CreateSpace Independent Publishing Platform, 2014.

Albom, Mitch. *Tuesdays with Morrie*. Doubleday, 1997. Revised version: Broadway books, 2007.

Alexander, William. *Flirting With French. How a Language Charmed Me, Seduced Me & Nearly Broke My Heart*. Algonquin Books of Chapel Hill, 2014.

Bacon, Roger. *Opus Tertium*. Brewer, 1214-1292.

Badinter, Elisabeth. *Le Conflit, la femme et la mère*. Flammarion, 2010. English version: *The Conflict: How Modern Motherhood Undermines the Status of Women*. Metropolitan Books, 2012.

Bhojwani, Malti. *The Mind Spa: Ignite Your Inner Life Coach*. Om Books International, 2015.

Boileau-Despréaux, Nicolas (often known simply as Boileau). *L'Art poétique*, Canto I. I. 1674.

Child, Julia. *My Life in France*. Prud'homme, 2006.

Cioran, Emil. *Aveux et anathèmes*. Gallimard-Arcades, 1987. English version: *Anathemas and Admirations*, Arcade Publishing, 2012.

Coelho, Paulo. *The Alchemist*. HarperCollins, 1993.

Couric, Katie. *The Best Advice I Ever Got; Lessons From Extraordinary Lives*. Random House, 2012. Quotes from her and also from: Beyoncé, Tony Bennett, Ina Garten, Billy Joel, Helen Mirren, Regis Philbin, Maria Elena Salinas, Eric Schmidt and Steven Spielberg.

Crafts, Leland W., Gilbert, Ralph W., Robinson, Elsa E., and Schneirla, Théodore C. *Recent Experiments in Psychology*. McGraw-Hill, 1950.

Druckerman, Pamela. *Bringing Up Bébé*. Penguin Books, 2012.

Etiemble, René. *Parlez-vous franglais ?* Gallimard Saint-Amand, 1964.

Franklin, Benjamin. *Poor Richard's Almanack*, 1736. New version: Thrift Editions, 1999.

La Fontaine, Jean de. *Fables, Livre Deuxième*, 1668.

Green, John & Levithan, David. *Will Grayson, Will Grayson*. Speak, 2011.

Green, Julien. *La Bouteille à la mer*. Gallimard, 1976.

Hale, Shannon. *The Goose Girl* (*The Books of Bayern*). Bloomsbury, 2005.

Hill, Napoleon. *Think and Grow Rich*. Fawcett Books, 1960.

Lee, Harper. *To Kill a Mockingbird*. Random House, 1960.

Mather, Philippe. *Stanley Kubrick at Look Magazine*. Intellect, 2013.

Michnick Golinkoff, Roberta, P h.D., and Hirsh-Pasek, Kathy. *How Babies Talk. The Magic and Mystery of Language in the First Three Years of Life*. Plume, 2000.

Mizubayashi, Akira. *Une langue venue d'ailleurs*. Gallimard, 2011.

Mori, Arimasa. *Notre-Dame dans le lointain*, 1967.

Murakami, Haruki. *After Dark*. Harvill Secker, 2007 & Vintage, Random House, 2008.

Muzyka, Zhena. *Life by the Cup*. Atria Paperback, 2014.

Nizard, Désiré. *Histoire de la littérature française (1844-1891)*. F. Didot Frères, Paris. 1854

Purkey, William W. *Becoming an Invitational Leader*, Humanix Books, 2002.

Senik, Claudia. *L'économie du bonheur*. Editions du Seuil, 2014.

Sharma, Robin.
> *Megaliving! 30 Days to a Perfect Life*. The Haunsla Corporation, 1994.
>
> *The Greatness Guide*. Harpers Collins, 2007.
>
> *The Monk Who Sold His Ferrari*. Harpers Collins, 1999.
>
> *Who Will Cry When You Die*. Harpers Collins, 2013.

Smith, Frank. *To Think: In Language, Learning and Education*. Teachers College Press, 1990.

Szasz, Thomas. *The Myth of Mental Illness*. Harper & Row, 1974.

Taylor, Erika. *Moving Forward*. Erika Ashby, 2014.

Thoreau, Henry David. *Walden*. Ticknor & Fields, 1854.

Wittgenstein, Ludwig. *Tractatus Logico-Philosophicus*, 1922.

II - ARTICLES

Alexander, William. "Learning a language as an adult is so hard. That's why it's so good for your brain." *The New York Times*, July 18, 2014.

Alladi, Suvarna, DM, Bak, Thomas H., MD, Duggirala, Vasanta, PhD, Bapiraju, Surampudi, PhD, Shailaja, Mekala, MA., Shukla, Anuj Kumar, MPhil, Chaudhuri, Jaydip Ray, DM, and Kaul, Subhash, DM. "Bilingualism delays age at onset of dementia, independent of education and immigration status." *Neurology*, November 26, 2013.

Audrerie, Sabine. "Le français est illogique, subtil, paradoxal, c'est sa richesse — Interview Philippe Delerm." *La Croix*, September 10, 2012.

Cohen, Ilisa. "Bilingual Babes: Teach Your Child A Second Language." *Parents Magazine*, circa 2012.

Cohen, Roger. "France's Glorious Malaise." Op-ed, *The New York Times*, July 11, 2013.

Craig, Jill. "Meet the French: cultural differences to be aware of when getting to know locals." *MyFrenchLife™*, October 21, 2015. www.myfrenchlife.org

Delistraty, Cody C. "For a Better Brain, Learn Another Language". Interview George Lakoff, a professor of cognitive science and linguistics at the University of California at Berkeley. *The Atlantic*, Washington DC, October 17, 2014.

Druckerman, Pamela. "On Mother's Day, Embrace Embarrassment." Op-ed, *The New York Times*, May 8, 2015.

"French Attracted to English Accent." *The Connexion*, May 14, 2015.

Greenhalf, Julia. "You know you're becoming more French when..." *MyFrenchLife™*, April 17, 2015. www.myfrenchlife.org

Harang, Florence. "Liberté, égalité, anxiété: Why are the French so pessimistic?" *My FrenchLife™*, June 9, 2015. www.myfrenchlife.org

Indivero, Victoria M. "Learning languages is a workout for brains, both young and old." *PennState News*, November 12, 2014.

Kinzler, Katherine. "The Superior Social Skills of Bilinguals." *The New York Times*, March 11, 2016.

Merzenich, Michael, Ph.D. "How You Can Make Your Brain Smarter Every Day." *Forbes*, August 6, 2013.

Ono-dit-Biot, Christophe. "Gérard Depardieu : "Toute ma vie, j'ai couru pour plaire." *Le Point*, October 7, 2014.

Roudaut, Christian. "Si douce France." *M Le Monde*, January 4, 2014.

Vitello, Paul. "They came, They Toured, They Offended," in which he quoted Steve Martin. *The New York Times*, May 27, 2007.

Weiler, Nicholas. "Speaking a second language may change how you see the world. "*Science Magazine*, March 17, 2015.

III. - BLOGS

Albrecht, Karl, Ph.D. "Change Your Words and Change Your World — How to stop using the language of powerlessness." September 15, 2014. www.BrainSnacks.com

Baudry, Pascal. www.pbaudry.com

Boutefeu, Jean-Louis. "Do you really want to learn French...? Or...?" Published on the website of the European Parliament in several languages: www.europarl.europa.eu

Bryant, Carroll. http://carrollbryant.blogspot.com/2012/09/quotes-by-carroll-bryant-vol-one.html

Brydges, Jenna. "Be Prepared For a New Personality When You Learn a New Language." www.techvalleyvonnect.com

C. JoyBell, C. http://cjoybellc.blogspot.com/2011/10/you-can-quote-me-1-30.html#.VTLGOpPzn48

Hwang Lynch, Grace. "Ways to Introduce Your Kids to Foreign Languages." PBS Parents. www.pbs.org

Kaufmann, Steve, founder of *LingQ*. www.lingq.com

Meyer, Judith. "13 Ways Language-learning Changes How You Think." www.learnLangs.com

Roopleen. Dr. http://drroopleen.com

Smith, Seth Adam. www.forwardwalking.com

Topel, Fred. "Olga Kurylenko leaves the runway for Quantum of Solace." November 11, 2008. www.craveonline.com

Young, Scott H. www.scotthyoung.com

IV - OTHERS

1. Speeches

Lewis, Flora. Address at the Round Table: *Dialogue Among Civilizations*. UNESCO, New York, September 2000.

Mendela, Nelson. Excerpts of what he said during some negotiations in the Apartheid era.

2. Music

Goldman, Jean-Jacques. *Il changeait la vie* (song). Album *Entre gris clair et gris foncé*. Epic Records, 1987. English translation by Grégoire Tricoire, 2013.

Renaud. *Putain de camion* (song, excerpts). Album *Putain de camion*. Virgin France, 1988.

Learn French at Home... But not alone!

Learn French at Home was created in August 2004 by a French native teacher and by a French professional in the communication field who both understand the challenges of learning another language and the difficulties of settling in a different culture. After many years of experience in teaching French in different countries, they designed a full range of French learning programs to assist any individual who wishes to learn French from their home or office. The lessons are given one-on-one and are totally personalized and customized to meet the learner's goals and objectives.

Since the lessons take place in the student's home or at the office, on Skype, it does not matter where the student lives, or travels. As of today, more than 3,000 students have put their trust in our French learning courses. Their feed-back demonstrates that they experience real and satisfying results, gain confidence, and succeed in speaking French with spontaneity.

www.learnfrenchathome.com
contact@learnfrenchathome.com